Kelly,

Life Lessons
For
Mia Rose

An Irreverent Guide to
Living and Loving Well

I♡ Rona is amazing. You too! Adore you xxx

CLAIRE FORDHAM

Love,
Claire x

ISBN: 1512070734
ISBN-13: 978-1512070736

For Mia Rose

CONTENTS

ACKNOWLEDGMENTS

It takes a village to raise a child. And another to write, edit and publish a book.

This book would not have been possible without my top team: Diane Aldred for copy editing, layout, all things Internet and friendship; Joan Scheibel for the classy cover design and friendship, Sheran James for her editing skill (especially correct use of semi-colons), advice, encouragement and friendship; Colin Ryan for first-pass editing, endless love and support; Max Cross for the cover photo of Mia Rose and, with Meci, thank you for bringing Mia Rose into our family; Mia Claire Cross for excellent notes on my first draft. If Mia Rose grows up to be half as splendid and inspiring as her namesake and her dad, then I'll be able to rest in peace. But not for a long while yet.

Special thanks to Julia Fordham and Marley Rose, and my parents Roy and Muriel Fordham for their longevity genes and topping our side of the family tree.

I am in awe of Mia Rose's other grandmother, Kelera Adimatoga, a stalwart of her village community in Fiji, who has raised five children of her own with her husband Isikeli Manasa Radolo and adopted another, Nemani. Kelera can catch enough fish with a single piece of string to feed her entire family, and is always available to babysit Mia Rose. Thanks also to Meci's siblings and cousin Ronnie for loving and playing with Mia Rose, and teaching her the importance of family by their fine example. Anita Chand, thank you so much for feeding and nurturing my Fiji family.

We are disparate and scattered, but we all love Mia Rose.

I am indebted to Cynthia Eller, Professor of Women's Studies and Religious Studies at Montclair University, New Jersey, for her insight and advice on the chapter about religion.

Thanks to Jamie Greene for the terrific testimonial. Pals Debi Brett, Simon Climie, Suzie Crowley, Steve Dennis, Nancy DiToro, Suzanne Donovan, Caroline Feraday, Simon Gluckman, Tina Jenkins, Lori Leve, Patricia Murphy, Loretta Muñoz, Kara Noble, Iggi Ogard, Laura Pallas, India Redman, Melanie Rothschild, Vonda Shepherd, Moira Steiner, Sue Turton, Tracey Ullman, John Watkin, Marilyn Wells, and Susanna Young.

This book is about family. Love and thanks to my favorite families: Aldred, Bigelow, Brand, Brook, Linehan-Cross, Darvill, Fine, Fordham, Frome, Garf, Gatfield, Gazaryants, Goldsmith, Greene, Gunn, Harrington, Hartley, Hildebrand, Jones, Ketterhagen, Kluge, McKell, McKeown, Morris, Oxford, Randall, Rice, Rona, Ryan, Smiley, Spruyt, Strongetham, Tarnay, Tedesco, Wasserman, Watkin, Wells, Young, and Young.

1

DEAR MIA ROSE

This book is my gift to you for your sixteenth birthday. I hope it will make you smile, be of comfort to you in times of trouble and provide a few handy tips on how to cope with the challenges of life.

Mostly, I want you to know me — warts and all. In Western culture, we know little if anything about our parents and grandparents, and how their experiences shaped their lives and the people they became. You might think that's a good thing once you've read this.

I may have been a little hasty when I said I would stop coloring my hair when I became a grandmother. That time has now come with your birth, but my colorist will still be seeing me once a month.

Forget about growing old gracefully, I am going to be dragged into my dotage kicking and screaming. There are so many adventures to be had, like more trips to Fiji, where you live with your mum and my son – your dad.

Photographs, FaceTime and Skype are all well and good, but I want to teach you to cook, swim, read, write, and play hide-and-seek in person.

Your parents told me that the first birthday and the sweet sixteenth of Fijian children are considered the most important and should be celebrated. Grand Poppa C (your step grandfather) and I flew to Fiji for your first birthday party. It was just incredible and we had the best time playing with you, singing to you and reading you stories. We'll be there for your sweet sixteenth and many times in between and after.

I hope you like me. Of course you will. I'm fun. Parents are annoying. But grandparents are fun, fluffy and kind. Or rather, we should be. And wise. Your dad and aunt chose to ignore most of my advice and words of wisdom, but they are happy, healthy and thriving, so I must have done something right.

One of the best things we can do for our children (apart from loving and feeding them, of course) is to set a good example and learn from our own parents' mistakes. My mother was unable to resist mentioning that she didn't like the name Marley that my sister chose for her daughter (your cousin once removed), as it reminded her of Marley's ghost in *A Christmas Carol* by Charles Dickens. I vowed never to be so tactless about my own children's choice of names for their offspring. Although I defy any Westerner not to raise an eyebrow when their son announces he is going to call his unborn child Vosamana, a Fijian name meaning: "what he says happens," if you turned out to be a boy.

In Fijian culture, it is the custom for the father to name the first-born. And the greatest honor is to have a child named after you. Your dad named you after his favorite person, his sister (my daughter), Mia. The child and the person they are named after call each other Yaca (pronounced yatha). To avoid confusion, I will refer to your aunt as Yaca in this book and you as Mia Rose.

Your dad wanted to name you Mia Claire to honor me as well, but that's Yaca's name and I suggested you should have your own identity. Mia Rose is an excellent compromise. I confess I breathed a sigh of relief when you were born a girl and we dodged the Vosamana bullet.

Another name that will keep cropping up is my sister, Julia, known as GAJ since you were born (short for Great Aunt Julia).

The Fijian word for the paternal grandmother is Bubu. That'll do nicely. I'm way too young to be a Grandma or Grannie. I see my three main roles as to ensure you are the best-dressed, best-educated and best-informed girl in Fiji. You are certainly dearly loved.

Grand Poppa C has never had children of his own and is almost as besotted with you as I am. He said it seems like the world is a different and better place since you were born. I'm glad he feels that way, because his Porsche fund is now your college kitty.

Maybe you'll pass this book on to your own daughter and granddaughter. Better yet, write one for them once you've lived and loved a bit.

Happy sixteenth birthday, Mia Rose.

I love you.

Always,

Bubu

xxxx

Family Tree

| Muriel Hulme
Great grandmother
+
Royston Fordham
Great grandfather | Elsa Rose Greene
Great grandmother
+
Edward Albert Cross
Great grandfather | Laitenai Tabusoli Nabose
Great grandmother
+
Waisale Waqanisau
Great grandfather | Moti Cokanasiga
Great grandmother
+
Isikeli Rogoivalu
Great grandfather |

| Claire Fordham
Grandmother
+
Martin Cross
Grandfather | Kelera Adimaitoga
Grandmother
+
Isikeli Manasa Radolo
Grandfather |

| Mia Claire Cross
Aunt | Max Cross
Father
+
Silameci Kelera
Mother |

Mia Rose

2

BRINGING UP BABY

All children are the not same and one style of parenting does not fit all. Babies are born with one of seven personality types: Shy, reckless, timid, fussy, happy, aggressive or anxious.

Most parents don't have the time, patience or wherewithal to tailor their parenting to each child's particular needs.

Even with the best parenting and high self-esteem, a person can still be devastated by a friend, teacher, colleague or lover who does or says the wrong thing. But the child with high self-esteem should be able to brush off criticisms and deal with painful break-ups and rejection more easily and quickly.

Your dad was a happy baby and an adorable child who, while accident-prone (I stopped counting after nineteen trips to the ER), did as he was told. If he ever was guilty of some minor misdemeanor, he confessed quickly, apologized sincerely and didn't do it again. Or at least wasn't caught.

He wasn't very good at going to bed or sleeping through the night and there was a time when I was concerned he would still be wearing diapers when he went for his first job interview. But I doted on him. He could do no wrong in my eyes, which is why Yaca (your aunt after whom you were named) sneeringly called him "The Golden Child" from the moment she could talk.

If your dad was born happy, Yaca was born feisty. Or aggressive, to use the technical term. Where your dad would say, "Yes, Mum" and smile, Yaca would snarl and give me a look that said, "Go fuck yourself." When she was a teenager, she would even say it out loud.

I don't know where she learned that foul language.

Yaca needed a different type of parenting from your dad. She needed even more love, confidence-building and patience from me than I was able to give in her early, formative years.

But let's start at the beginning. Babies just need breast milk or formula if you can't breastfeed for the first four – six months and on demand, then puréed vegetables and fruit for the first year. No meat or fish until twelve months and even then only in moderation.

I used to boil up fresh vegetables for my babies and purée them, then freeze any leftovers for emergencies. I'd like to say I never gave them processed food, but I'm sure there were a couple of times that I must have if we were out of the good stuff.

I've seen mothers give their babies sweetened tea and coffee in a bottle — so wrong, on so many levels.

I breastfed your dad for his first twelve months. I'd have stopped sooner, but he didn't want me to. Once a child starts walking, it looks weird to me to see them being breastfed. I didn't make so much milk with Yaca and had to abandon breastfeeding after about four months.

These are just a few tips I can offer from what I have learned the hard way to help you bring up a happy and healthy child. Most importantly, you will learn from the mistakes I made as a parent and save you and your children a lot of heartache. Take what you like from my list and leave the rest.

The most important thing we can do for our children is to set a good example. Not to be so brilliant and successful that they are always in your shadow, but to live by a certain moral code that knows right from wrong. Most attitudes and beliefs are learned behavior. If you are a racist, a bully, violent or abusive, the chances are your child will be too.

I was a full-time mum until Yaca started school, so I had the time and energy to give your dad and Yaca my full attention. When they woke up in the night, I went to them, fed them, changed their diaper/nappy and cuddled them back off to sleep. Even when Yaca came along and I was exhausted with another young child and a home to run, I took care of her every need.

No nanny or housekeeper.

Once you have a second child, you're so tired, impatient and often broke that you start shouting instead of asking nicely and calmly. So tensions can run high.

Disposable diapers had only just come into fashion when your dad was born, so I did what my mum did and used towel nappies that needed to have the poo scraped off (it took a while for me to discover nappy liners), then to be soaked in a bucket before being washed on a high heat (at least I had a washing machine) and, if the sun was shining or there was a nice breeze, hung out on a washing line.

I was lucky and had a tumble drier when the weather was bad (more often than not in England), but my mum instilled in me the importance of drying clothes on a washing line if at all possible. My mum didn't even have a washing machine when I was born. She boiled my nappies in a bucket on the stove.

I soon worked out that drying nappies in the tumble drier was the way to go as it keeps them softer. Another reason I didn't like your dad's nappies drying outside is that the first time I washed them, I had left a brown pillowcase in the machine that turned my beautiful white nappies a nasty shade of beige and I was too ashamed to hang them out for the neighbors to notice. Seeing my bright white nappies ruined and so soon was deeply upsetting at the time.

When Yaca came along, I used the same nappies. My mother also taught me the importance of thrift and good housekeeping.

I still remember clearly the day when I was changing Yaca's nappy on the bathroom floor and your dad was peeing in the toilet but missed and peed over me, which caused me to shriek and lose concentration, allowing Yaca's left foot to escape my grip and land in her massive poo, which made me cry out again in despair, startling your dad so he knocked over the full nappy bucket that covered me and the carpet in stinky poo water. I cried as I scraped the poo from between Yaca's toes.

Poo is a recurring theme in my worst times. When your dad and Yaca were young, I didn't allow them candy or sodas except on special occasions. By the way, if I had my time over again, I would never give my children soda. I saw a commercial on TV for a new sugarless wonder mint and thought this would be an excellent compromise for sweets.

What I didn't know was that the replacement the manufacturers used for sugar was sorbitol, an artificial sweetener known by everyone but me for its laxative properties. I happily gave Yaca and your dad a packet each to munch on while we drove to the new local Olympic-sized swimming pool for a fun family day out.

Family Guy is your dad and Yaca's favorite cartoon. There's often a scene where Stewie or Brian spew gallons of puke for minutes at a time. That's how your dad and Yaca shat. It went everywhere and just wouldn't stop.

It started when they were in the pool, so the pool had to be drained. Lifeguards were gagging, other swimmers were screaming as they clambered out of the water. The shit just kept pouring out of them even as we raced off to the changing rooms. We didn't go back to the pool for many years in case we were recognized.

There were many happy and fun times during your dad and Yaca's childhood. I have the photographs to prove it. But tragedy plus time equals comedy and no one wants to read about what a brilliant, albeit slightly shouty and impatient mother I was and how happy for the most part their childhood years were for me. But the teenage years… yikes.

Some parents are so exhausted they resort to what's called Ferberizing their babies, named after Dr. Richard Ferber who advocated letting babies cry for specific amounts of time when you put them to bed until they get the message that you won't be coming and they fall asleep. Eventually. Allegedly.

I just knew in my gut that was a bad idea. Maybe if I had to go to work the next day I might have thought differently, but when babies are left to cry for long periods, a fight-or-flight response sets in and the child harbors a feeling of never having their needs met. Ferberized kids often grow up to be angry, resentful and fearful or withdrawn and miserable. I can usually spot a Ferberized kid.

Dr. Ferber himself now acknowledges that all families are different and even recommends co-sleeping as being best for some babies. That's the natural Fijian way. That's going too far in the opposite direction for me — I'm a light sleeper.

Once your dad could get out of bed himself, he would just climb into bed with me and Grandpa. I gave up trying to get him to stay in his own bed after six months of gentle, patient persuasion.

I think that's why I was so frustrated with Yaca's resentment towards me because she was never left to cry and her needs as a baby were always met. She was a fantastic sleeper, though. Still is.

If you have a crying baby, it's OK to let them suck on a pacifier once in a while. When I was pregnant with your dad, my mum told me it was a terrible mistake to give babies a pacifier (or dummy as we called them in the UK) because it takes forever to wean them off. Your dad never needed one, but I think both Yaca and I would have benefitted from her having one to stop her crying, even for five minutes.

It is not OK to hit your child, however shitty their behavior might be and exhausted you are. Ideally, we shouldn't shout at our kids either, but I think that's expecting a bit much if you have two. Consistency is vital in parenting but, again, that's easier said than done when you're tired. Once a parent relents when they've said "no" to television or ice cream, it's all over and the child has won. The kid knows the parent can be broken and will beg and scream for hours until the parent gives in again.

That's why it's a good idea not to have more than two children. Parents should never be outnumbered. I also believe that it's not possible to meet the intellectual and emotional needs of more than two.

The best advice I can give you about parenting is to listen to your children, especially during their teenage years. If they are angry and upset about moving up to London when they didn't want to go at aged fourteen, don't spend hours explaining why they are wrong to feel that way. Listen and hear them. Chances are they'll soon come around as long as they know you understand that they aren't happy about it rather than telling them to stop those negative feelings.

When you are in the wrong, be able to say, "I am sorry. Please forgive me. I love you."

Kids don't like it when their parents break up. So do yourself a favor and before you commit to having a child with someone, try, as best you can, to pick someone who doesn't have any deal-breaking habits.

Don't go for the movie-star good looks, go for kind and thoughtful. Of course, there must be chemistry, but you want a guy who shows up when he says he will, loves you unconditionally, is creatively fulfilled but understands the need to earn a living.

That doesn't mean to say you are looking for a man to support you. Oh no. You need to be financially independent and have a career of your own. But if you have to take time off work to have a baby that you both want, then he might have to bear the brunt of paying the bills for a while. If you have chosen a guy who would rather buy a season ticket to watch his favorite football team than diapers and food for the baby, you're in for some heartache. Likewise, you will have to put designer handbags and shoes on hold for a while. Possibly forever.

It's a miracle to me when any marriage lasts with the exhaustion and financial struggles that raising children usually entails. Throw in an infidelity and a job loss and sometimes it seems easier to give up. Then you swap one set of problems for another.

If you do end up being a single parent, it is not OK to have boyfriends sleep over when your children are in the house. And don't move another man in unless you are absolutely sure the kids are cool with it.

Men rarely actually like other men's children and, even if they say they do, they'd rather they weren't in the picture. Kids pick up on that. In the animal kingdom, many male species (particularly lions) kill their stepchildren as soon as they hook up with the mother.

Most of Yaca's issues with me could be traced back to the divorce. Again this was frustrating to me, as I maintained a good relationship with her dad, your grandpa. He was and still is very much involved in their lives. We attended all school events together and birthday parties, even a couple of family weddings.

When a therapist here in the US told me how divorce seriously impacts children, I scoffed. "That's ridiculous," I said. "Most couples I know have broken up. If what you are saying is true, there must be thousands of messed-up teenagers out there."

"Yes, there are," she said. "That's why so many teenagers join gangs. It gives them a sense of family they often don't get at home."

That same therapist once told me that there is only one type of client she would never take on: a woman who chose to bring a baby into the world without the support of a loving partner. Because bringing up a child is such a hard job if you do it properly. And it's isolating, so the single mother is usually severely depressed at some point.

While I think it's true the vast majority of parents would agree that having children is the best and most fulfilling thing they ever did (with only a few exceptions), I don't think children enhance a marriage. They bring so much responsibility and opportunities for conflict.

What I mean is that if you are in a relationship with problems, they will only be exacerbated with the advent of children. So never think for one moment that having a baby will make everything OK.

You may well be so successful and financially secure by the time you decide to have a family that money will not be an object, which will put you in the top one percent of the population. I want you to know that it's fine to be ordinary and just have a regular job. There's too much pressure on people to be extraordinary these days.

However, if you and your partner are like most of the world and live on a fixed budget, your children's needs must be met before your own. I totally judge people who spend what little money they have on beer and cigarettes when their kids need food and clothing.

Bringing up children is the most important job in the world. But it can be a tad boring to be stuck at home all day waiting for your family to come in from school or work. And your life can be one endless round of shopping, cleaning, washing and cooking.

There's also the danger that if you devote your life to raising a family full time, you will lose your mind with Empty Nest Syndrome when they leave home, feel your life has passed you by and find that you are no longer employable.

Babies sleep a lot during the day, so even though you'll be glad to nap and recharge your batteries, you might find you are eager to get back to work, especially if you have a great job to go back to.

Ideally, a mother of young children will work part-time so she can earn some extra money, have some adult conversation, a creative outlet or job fulfillment and not be so exhausted that she doesn't have time or energy for her kids when she gets in from work.

Again, ideally, a relative or trusted family friend will look after your kids while you are at work, someone who can be a loving, consistent presence and a good influence on their lives.

If you are a working mother, try to have dinner together as a family at least five nights a week.

I've been lucky that I was able to work mostly from home when my children were small. Grandpa's mum was my main helper when I needed them picking up from school.

I only forgot to collect my children from school once, when I was engrossed in an article I was writing for the *Dorset Mail*. Luckily, Mrs. Hill (Yaca's kindergarten teacher) waited at the school gates with them until I got there. I was half an hour late. These days in the US, parents get fined if they are even five minutes late collecting their kids from school.

An upsetting experience as a parent (that didn't involve poo) was when I dropped Yaca off at tennis camp and was sure I could drive to the next town to interview someone for the *Dorset Evening Echo* and get back in plenty of time to collect her. I didn't take into account there were road works coming back that slowed traffic to a crawl. This was in the days before cell phones, so I couldn't call anyone to pick her up for me and I didn't pass a public telephone.

I was frantic by the time I got there, almost an hour late. Yaca still brings that up to this day. She forgets the bit about Ben and Joe Lever's mum staying with her until I got there so she was never in any danger. The way she tells it, she barely escaped being kidnapped and murdered and has been emotionally scarred by the childhood trauma of being forgotten and abandoned by her mother that terrible day at tennis camp.

You have been blessed with wonderful parents. Not because he's my son, but I have never seen a more hands-on and loving father than yours. Your mum too. It brought a tear to my eye to watch and listen to them singing to you when you were a tiny baby and they used to change your diaper every hour so you didn't get nappy rash.

That lasted about two months. Incidentally, Aveeno diaper rash cream is the best. Over two years, I must have posted about ten tubes to Fiji.

I'm not sure who benefitted most from Anita being in your life: you or your mum. Anita is your dad's cook and housekeeper who became your nanny when you were born. Anita or your mum would massage you with coconut oil twice a day.

Anita and Nau (your other grandmother) have been your mum's main helpers with you. I wish I lived closer so I could have helped her more. I don't think I have ever seen a happier, more wanted and loved child than you.

You have just the right amount of "don't mess with me" attitude that I am confident you will grow up with the highest possible self-esteem and that no one will dare mess with you. But don't worry, if you get too self-important and have even the slightest sense of entitlement, I'll be there to bring you down a peg or too. Although I did read somewhere that having a sense of entitlement does instill a confidence that is helpful in the job market.

I tell you, parenting is a minefield. Everything we say and do and everything we don't say and don't do can have an enormous impact on our children.

The important thing is that they all feel equally loved and parents don't show favoritism. According to a recent study, sixty percent of parents admit to having a favorite child and the other forty percent are just good at hiding it.

Then, if your children reach adulthood knowing and feeling that they were and are the most important people in your life (apart from that one day at tennis camp), that you will do everything and anything you can to help them be happy, healthy and live their best possible life, they might even like you when they grow up and enjoy spending time with you, even if they hated you when they were teenagers, which they probably will.

My absolute greatest pleasure in life is when your dad and Yaca Skype or FaceTime me, which they do every week without being asked. And they pay for their own flights to come and see me in LA once a year. So I think it's fair to say we are a close family.

I couldn't be more proud of them both. My relationship with Yaca is brilliant and beyond my wildest dreams. She is my confidante, my joy, the funniest, kindest, most remarkable person I have ever known and my current favorite child. Although, since your birth, the scales are edging back in your dad's direction.

Life Lesson # 1 *Family is everything so call your parents at least once a week after you leave home and your grandparents every two weeks.*

Recommended further reading: *The Mother Dance: How Children Change Your Life* by Harriet Lerner, *The Pecking Order: Which Siblings Succeed and Why* by Dalton Conley, *Becoming Attached: First Relationships and How They Shape Our Capacity to Love* by Robert Karen.

3

THE POINT?

When I held your dad in my arms for the first time on April 7, 1979 and wished only the best for him, I never imagined that he would live in Fiji and you, my first grandchild would be born an ocean away.

The first time he went to Fiji was in 2004. He went to Savusavu for a month to build a small recording studio for a friend of GAJ's. He said it was the best time of his life. He loved the people and the pace and quality of life there which was much less frenetic than London or Los Angeles.

Eight years later, when he was at a crossroads in his life and living with me and Grand Poppa C in LA, we discussed all his possibilities (endless, as he had no responsibilities) and he remembered that the most content he had ever been was that month in Fiji. Then, as often happens in life when you really want something, an opportunity arose for him to return there for five days.

He did and never left. It turned out to be the best decision he ever made.

Friends and family have often pitied me that my son, and now you as well, live so far away but I don't see it that way. How could I not be happy that my child is happy and that you both live in paradise with your mum and Fiji family?

As I write this, you are three years old. I've been to Fiji three times to see you and you've been here to LA twice.

I want us to have a good and authentic relationship, so when your friends ask about your English grandmother and wonder what she is (or was) like, you will know. Of course, there's a danger you will answer, "Strange and self-absorbed. Can you believe she wrote me a book? About herself. For my sixteenth birthday. I'd have preferred a car."

This is also an opportunity for me to reflect on my life so far as I begin Act Three of this incredible journey we call life. We may both learn something.

I wouldn't mind discovering the meaning of life and the point of it all myself. I have been wondering for a while.

Self-help, positive-thinking gurus (I've read them in my ongoing quest to live my best possible life) recommend writing down how you want your life to be within five years, putting it in the present tense as if it has already happened, otherwise it will be part of your future and not your present.

I have a book at the back of a cupboard somewhere in which I wrote affirmations (when I believed that we create our own reality with our thoughts) and my "within five years" wishes.

Found it. Here we are. This was written on April 6, 2001.

I am happily married to a man I love, like and respect (tick). *He loves likes and respects me* (tick). *It's a loving, caring, sharing, trusting relationship* (tick). *We are the most important person in each other's life* (tick). *My children are happy, healthy, loving, loveable and living their best possible lives* (tick). *I have a rewarding, fulfilling and successful career in writing and television* (meh). *I am rich* (could not be further from the truth). *Lack of money is never a problem for me* (laughing through the tears). *I make TV programs and write books and articles* (tick). *I am involved in the film industry* (ish). *I am able to afford nice clothes* (sales only), *a good, reliable car* (tick), *have regular holidays with and without my children* (tick). *I can buy all that I need for myself, friends and family* (tick). *My husband is successful and happy in his career and supportive to me in mine* (tentative tick). *We live in a large, comfortable house with a beautiful garden filled with trees and flowers* (even though we live in an apartment, it is part of a large and comfortable house, GAJ's, that has a beautiful garden filled with trees and flowers so this is, technically, a tick). *The house is full of laughter and happiness, love and music. It attracts good people who warm to the atmosphere of love* (big, fat tick). *Children are welcome* (bigger, fatter tick). *There is no bitterness or resentment in my life, only health* (tick), *wealth* (nope), *love* (yep), *happiness* (yep) *creativity* (tick). *Mine is the happiest of families* (tick). *All is well in my world* (tick).

I'm realizing, as I try and write an honest picture of how my life is, that while my bank account doesn't runneth over and rarely has, I do live an extraordinarily privileged life because I am, without doubt, the luckiest person I know and do attract supremely successful and wealthy people and amazing opportunities into my orbit.

I have stayed in some of the finest hotels in the world, eaten at the finest restaurants, won Wimbledon Center Court tickets in the public ballot, gone to Ladies' Day at Ascot and bet on a horse in the last race that romped home at 100/1, drunk champagne out of the Cheltenham Gold Cup, travelled first class to Japan and The Philippines (thanks to GAJ's success as a singer-songwriter) and Grand Poppa C and I were married at Cecil B. DeMille's former home in Los Feliz courtesy of kind and generous friends. I did most of the catering for the hundred guests myself and it was a wonderful wedding.

I notice that I wrote my wish list on April 6, 2001. That's Grand Poppa C's birthday and we weren't even dating then.

My intention is to cover important subjects and to dispense as much sound advice as possible that might help ease your life's journey. I'm not going to lie to you, life is invariably hard for everyone at least some of the time.

The important things to know are that the worst of times will pass and there's usually something positive and lessons to be learned from even our darkest days.

Life Lesson # 2 *Goals are wishes with deadlines. Write down what you'd like to accomplish within five years, writing in the present tense as if it's already happened. You'll be surprised how much of it comes true.*

4

EDUCATION

All the problems in the world come from ignorance. Education is the only way to make the planet a better place, so learn as much as you possibly can about everything.

If you are good at languages, learn another language or three. You already knew some Hindi and Fijian by the time you were three, so I suspect you have a skill in that area. Chances are that Chinese might be big when you're sixteen. Being able to speak Mandarin Chinese could come in handy if you are in business, banking or politics.

For many young people, college years are one long opportunity to binge on sex, drink and drugs. Please, don't be stupid and make this phase of your life count. Because although a degree may not be worth much by the time you graduate, it will still be worth something and will be much better than nothing. Employers here in America often don't consider people for even the lowliest positions if they don't have a degree.

Develop a thirst for knowledge. If you don't know what you want to do for a career by the time you start university, study English. If you want to be a nurse, doctor or teacher (all worthy professions, by the way) then study the relevant subjects.

Don't waste your time posting too many selfies on whatever social media might be the trend, use your time on the Internet to research things you're interested in. There has to be some form of formal education, because the standard of English grammar on the web can be terrible. But there's so much free information available out there and it's mostly fascinating.

A university education is expensive, but we have a family motto: *There's always a way.* Harvard University has many free online courses and www.khanacademy.org is an extraordinary resource. It was established in 2006 by Salman Khan to provide a free, world-class education for anyone, anywhere.

Don't listen to the argument that subjects like, say, algebra, won't benefit you in later life. Sure, not everyone uses algebra every day, but it does teach you to think in terms of concepts and logical steps. Consider it mental gymnastics that will get your mind fit and open to different ways of thinking. If you have inherited a propensity for math and science, you didn't get it from your dad's side of the family.

My side isn't entrepreneurs or inventors, either. Maybe you will break the mold and discover or invent the next big thing. Just do something you love.

Absorb as much as you can and be interested in learning. Read. There's a difference between being able to read and being a reader. Your dad and Yaca are avid readers, but it took years to for them to get into the habit and actually enjoy it. Yaca loves a murder mystery.

I enjoy reading biographies. It can be inspiring and motivating to learn from other peoples' successes and mistakes. The most successful people in all walks of life have always encountered failure and rejection on their journey. It's how we cope with disappointment and rejection that defines our path and teaches us humility.

Watch commencement addresses on YouTube. They can be highly educational and so inspiring. My favorites are by JK Rowling, Steve Jobs and John Legend. Check them out.

I'll end this chapter with a quote from John Legend's 2014 commencement address at the University of Pennsylvania. It is excellent advice:

"Love your self, love your work, love the people around you. *Dare* to love those who are different from you, no matter where they're from, what they look like, and who they love. Pursue this life of love with focus and passion and ambition and courage. Give it your all. And that will be your path to true success."

Life Lesson # 3   *Learn something new every day.*

5

LOOKING GOOD

I'm not exaggerating when I say you were the most beautiful baby I've ever seen. There's a photo on my wall of your dad holding you when you were just twenty minutes old. He looks so happy and proud. He's looking at the camera and you are looking straight at him. Well, it looks like you are, but it takes a while for babies to be able to focus and even a baby as smart as you couldn't actually see at twenty minutes old. Nevertheless, I love that photo for capturing the first bonding experience between you and your dad.

I have a friend who looks great. She always wears makeup and dresses well. She told me once she realized she wasn't pretty, she also realized this meant she had to be extra-smart to make it in this world, so she studied extra-hard at school.

What she doesn't have in natural beauty, she makes up for with a terrific haircut, stylish clothes, great complexion, clever makeup and a fabulous smile, so when people see her they still go, "Wow."

The important thing is to make the best of what you have. Of course, it's also important to study hard so you can have a career you love that will pay a decent salary and enable you to have choices in life.

I had hoped to have been successful enough that I could have set you up with a trust fund so you wouldn't have to take shitty jobs until you find the career of your dreams. But it's probably a good thing I'm not. You will have a great sense of achievement and not the awful sense of entitlement so many spoiled rich kids have because they haven't had to work so hard.

Chances are at some point you will have to go on a job interview where first impressions count. I have heard many employers say how applicants who smile and are articulate are most likely to get the job. You have a great smile.

There are few things worse than a fake smile. Your smile must be natural and heartfelt. You have a happy disposition and are always smiling when I see you on Skype, so I am quietly confident you will take it with you to adulthood — barring tragedy and a bout of surly cow syndrome in your teenage years, of course.

Be careful not to overdo makeup. Less is more. I only wear lipstick, mascara, blemish hider (when needed) and a light foundation on special occasions. I am too lazy to wear full makeup every day and, anyway, a natural look is best I think. But because I wear lipstick, it looks like I make an effort.

A firm handshake is essential. Your dad and Yaca used to laugh at me when I made them practice their handshakes, but I think they will tell you that it has held them in good stead. And look the person in the eye when you shake their hand or greet them. We'll practice that when you're older.

I am quick to judge someone who has a weak handshake or can't look me in the eye and so are most people I know. There's only one person on earth who is allowed to have a limp handshake and that is the Queen of England. The Queen shakes so many hands she'd have a Repetitive Stress Injury if she was too firm every time.

It's not beyond the realms of possibility that you will be the first bi-racial member of the British Royal Family and we'll deal with that handshake dilemma if/when we get to it.

Accepting that you will be articulate, charming, confident, witty, smiling and firm of hand, let's start at the top and work down:

My daughter has fabulous hair — long, lustrous and thick. Apart from the time she cut it short when she was in her teens and put thick, blonde stripes in it, her hair has always looked amazing. Some have even called it her best feature. Which is saying something, because until you were born, hers was the most beautiful face I'd ever seen. Yaca has hair from her father's side of the family.

A great haircut is well worth the investment. Find a good hairdresser and stick with him or her. If all else fails, you can wear a stylish hat.

You will need a hat or two once your hair starts going grey and you suffer the indignity of root re-growth. Hopefully, by the time your hair starts going grey, they will have isolated that troublesome gene and you will never know the expense of monthly visits to a hair colorist.

I can tell already that you have a lovely complexion. Let's keep it that way.

And here's how. Drink plenty of water and DON'T SMOKE! Smoking ages the skin. Check out the complexion of the middle-aged smokers you know, if they're still alive. They will look much older than non-smokers and the few teeth they have left will be brown, if not black. Very much like their lungs.

One of the best and cheapest ways to ensure a clear and glowing complexion is to drink hot water with lemon. Squeeze half a lemon in a large cup or mug, put a splash of cold water in so as not to destroy the vitamin C when you top up with hot water. I try to drink a cup every day. I can see the difference if I miss one day.

Everyone has different skin and you will need to try different products before you find the range that suits you best. Coconut oil is an excellent moisturizer for the face and body, plenty of that in Fiji.

GAJ, Yaca and I used Clinique products for years. Their three-step program is excellent. Do not skimp on the second stage (toning) like I did until this year to save money. Yaca pointed out the error of my ways and I have noticed an improvement once I started toning. You are never too old to learn. Yaca also got me to switch from the bar of soap to their liquid soap.

There's a relatively new step that involves a serum. All beauty experts agree we must cleanse, tone and then moisturize. Clinique recommends using their serum after you moisturize, but I switched to the Jason range of moisturizers and used the Clinique serum before I moisturized with Jason.

I've recently switched again (you have to shake it up) to Neutrogena products and not just because they are cheap. Neutrogena consistently comes out top in best beauty product lists.

My favorite serum, the most critically acclaimed and the cheapest, is Protect & Perfect by No. 7 — available in Target in the United States and Boots in the United Kingdom.

And a good eye cream is vital once you're twenty-five. Neutrogena is working for me and is much cheaper than Strivectin eye cream, which I also like and find effective.

I take a daily fish oil called Imedeen that I swear by. It would probably be cheaper to have a facelift, but I found when I stopped taking it a few years back there was a dramatic increase in wrinkles. I won't be making that mistake again.

I expect the brands I have mentioned will still be around in ten years or so when you should start moisturizing, or perhaps there will be a magic pill to keep you young and beautiful when you're my age. Let's hope so.

I hope it doesn't, but the day may come when you have to go on an economy drive to save money on what some may consider a luxury, although I consider face creams a necessity. If that time comes, it is OK to go to the Clinique counter and ask if they have any samples you could try, pretending you might become a new customer if you like it. Just to tide you over, you understand.

I've just started using a few drops of lavender oil combined with a dime-sized blob of Vitamin E oil as a cleanser. I massage it into my face at night and wipe it off with a hot, wet face cloth. Then Neutrogena day and night creams. They seem to be working quite well.

Another "no" for the complexion is sugar. It makes you fat, rots your teeth, causes diabetes *and* gives you spots. Every spot I get comes after I've eaten chocolate, ice cream or candy. By the way, the best remedy for a spot is to dab it with tea tree oil when you feel one coming. It will usually disappear before it comes to a horrible head.

If you are plagued with acne and nothing better has been invented, try Proactiv. It's another three-step program and it really works.

I still use it once a week, now in my late fifties, to make sure I don't get spots. The annoying thing about Proactiv is you have to send away for it and the manufacturer locks you in to a six-weekly repeat order. They say you can cancel at any time, but most customers end up with much more than they need. There are dispensers, but they're few and far between. There's one at the shopping mall in Westwood. That was a happy day when I came across it by accident. Proactiv is not horribly expensive. In fact, it's quite reasonably priced. I just wish they'd sell it in shops. I will get it for you if you ever need it.

Zinc is a good mineral supplement if you are prone to spots. And it fends off colds as well. Eat plenty of fresh fruit and vegetables as part of your health and beauty regimen. Every day. There is no downside.

When you get older, the first thing to go is your neck. My neck isn't bad for my age and that's because I do a daily neck exercise and have done since I was thirty-five. It involves making a hideously unattractive face by jutting out your lower jaw repeatedly. I will show it to you when we are alone. This must never be done in front of a husband or boyfriend, but it must be done.

One of the few advantages of not being rich is that I have never been able to afford a facelift. That said, I am thinking about saving up for a little mini-lift. Just a little nip and tuck of jowl and neck. And only one. I promise.

The big thing today is laser treatment that all the movie stars claim they have instead of a facelift. It's said to be good for the complexion too. One day.

It is the lesser of two evils to take bits out, I think. I wouldn't put any Botox in. It might start off looking OK, even great, at first. But regular use will eventually make you look frozen and just plain wrong. And it's crazy expensive. The money would be better spent on your grandchildren's education.

I did try Restylane once. It's a filler that's injected under the eye to improve puffiness and dark circles. Allegedly. It didn't work for me as, I now know, I have very sensitive skin around my eyes. In fact it went horribly wrong. I had two black eyes that took two weeks to clear, massive swelling and a big scab where the needle went in. Lesson learned.

There will probably be something about your appearance you don't like at some point. Just don't obsess about it. As someone once said, it's our imperfections that make us beautiful. That sounds a lot better than the reality and was probably made up to comfort someone's grandchild who had a facial deformity.

The thing I hate most about my appearance is my eyebrows. Mine are too thin and not long enough and a good pair helps shape the face. Before I went the permanent make-up route, I investigated other options.

I visited the premises of one Anastasia in Beverly Hills. Not only is she probably the world's most expensive eyebrow plucker, Anastasia sells a range of products she claims will give us eyebrows to be proud of.

An assistant offered to demonstrate their most popular products. She found a template of the perfect brow for me after measuring angles and doing various calculations. I loved it that someone was taking my plight so seriously.

Twenty minutes and $122 later, I left the store with Anastasia's Essential Brow Kit and the thickest powdered on eyebrows since Joan Crawford (Hollywood actress from the 1940s). I wasn't fooling anyone. They screamed "fake."

An avalanche of tweezers, brushes and powders later – enough to open my own brow boutique – I thought I finally devised an essential kit that worked for me: a sable brush, Merle Norman's Storm powder, slanted tweezers by Tweezerman and a 10X magnifying mirror. But they kept fading and smudging so now I have a pair of eyebrows tattooed on and they don't look half bad - much better than the bald, smudged alternative anyway.

Just when I thought all was well in my own private beauty parlor and was able to smile smugly that I had cracked my great brow conundrum, I caught a glimpse in my magnifying mirror of what appeared to be the makings of a moustache.

Not as spectacular as Mexican artist Frida Kahlo's fantastic face fungus that she wore so proudly in the 1940s, but an issue that needed addressing, and sharpish. You have to ask yourself: if Frida had done something about her upper lip follicles, would Diego Rivera still have jumped into bed with her sister who didn't have a grassy grin?

Soon, the magnifying mirror (with which I have become obsessed) revealed a veritable bush of nose hair. And then, as I plunged the depth of human misery, the day dawned when tweezers wasn't enough to deal with upper lip or chin hair and I had to get out the big guns: laser hair removal.

Here's something they don't always tell you at the beauty parlor: Laser hair removal only works on dark hair, not grey or white.

Use the money you won't be wasting on cigarettes for laser hair removal on your underarm and legs and, if necessary, in the place discreetly referred to as the bikini line.

In the meantime, I recommend Veet cream for leg hair removal. It lasts for days and doesn't feel stubbly.

GAJ and Yaca have promised to pluck my 'tash and beard for me if I am ever in a coma and unable to do it myself. I've told them not to worry about my legs since no one will see them under the sheets.

One last bit of beauty advice. Obviously, my hope is that you will always feel comfortable in your own skin, but if you ever meet another woman who looks incredible, ask her to share her beauty secrets with you.

I'd be very surprised if surgery, liposuction, chemical peels and quite a lot of money aren't involved with the best looking women. The only thing stopping me from going down that route, apart from better things to do with my money, is setting a good example for you and Yaca.

I don't want either of you to feel you aren't pretty enough as you are. As singer-songwriter Joni Mitchell said, "Happiness is the best facelift."

Life Lesson #4   *Don't leave home without lipstick or lip gloss in your purse but it's bad manners to apply it at the dinner table.*

Recommended further reading: *The Tao of Beauty* by Helen Lee.

6

SEX

This chapter will have to be brief, as I suspect your dad is huddled in a fetal position with his fingers in his ears, rocking to and fro, trying to think of a happy place until he's sure you've finished reading it.

My hope is that you are aged sixteen as you read this, so you should know something about sex, even if you haven't tried it yet. I hope you haven't for several reasons, not least because girls who have had their first sexual experiences before sixteen have an increased risk of cervical cancer (a sexually transmitted disease, believe it or not) if they have sex with a male infected with the Human Papillomavirus (HPV) because their vagina isn't ready for sex and is more likely to absorb the virus.

There's a vaccination available now to protect against HPV and we should know soon whether it's effective without horrible and long-term side effects. But better to be safe than sorry and insist the guy wears a condom. They also help protect you from other sexually transmitted diseases and unplanned pregnancy.

It's actually quite difficult to get pregnant, as there are only a few days in a female's menstrual cycle when she can conceive. But the law of sod applies more to sex than almost anything else, which means if you don't want to get pregnant and you have unprotected sex, you probably will get pregnant. So, for goodness sake, use a condom.

It is my fervent wish that you will know the joy of great sex before you are twenty-five and for many years to come (no pun intended), hopefully with a man or woman who you love and who loves you, because sex can be amazing. It can be a truly extraordinary experience.

Some people can take it or leave it. Some people are repulsed by the very idea. It can be messy and occasionally painful, but it can be so mind-blowingly wonderful that you want to run up a mountain afterwards singing "The Hills Are Alive With The Sound Of Music," or the modern equivalent.

So, unless you are forced to have sex against your will, please know that sex is not a dirty word. It is to be enjoyed best with a loving partner. However, don't work in the sex industry and use your body to earn money either as a stripper, pole dancer, porn star or prostitute. Your friends and family will still love you, but they won't respect you for it and you would most likely be full of self-loathing at some point in your career, probably when your kids start school.

Out of love and respect for your parents and the bounds of good taste, I will not discuss orgasm or masturbation — except to share my favorite masturbation joke: the great thing about masturbation is that you don't have to look your best.

Life Lesson # 5   *Condoms are your friend.*

Recommended further reading: *The Tao of Health, Sex & Longevity: A Modern Practical Guide to the Ancient Way* by Daniel P. Reid.

7

LABOR OF LOVE

Around 134 million babies are born every year and the chances are good that you probably won't die during childbirth. But 275,000 girls and women do. Even if you don't die, it really bloody hurts.

There will most likely be a time during the proceedings when you wish for death or the slow and painful demise of the man who made you pregnant. There can be complications and infection could set in even if you survive labor and childbirth. And woe betide any girl or woman who doesn't do her pelvic floor exercises after her baby's born as it's a given you will be a pant-pisser by the time you are forty-five, if not before.

Pelvic floor exercises (sometimes called Kegels) involve clenching your vagina and rectum for five seconds then relax for five seconds. Repeat six times every day. You can do it while standing or lying down.

The most accurate description of childbirth I have heard is that it's like shitting a football. British singer Robbie Williams said being at the messy end when his daughter was born was like watching his favorite pub burn down.

The point being that it's a war zone down there, during and (for a while) after childbirth. I have a theory that it's no place for a man and wonder if the soaring divorce rates in the Seventies started when it became fashionable for men to be present during the delivery process.

Men often say witnessing the birth of their babies is the most amazing experience of their lives and they wouldn't have missed it for the world. But I have had more than a few male colleagues and friends confide that they never felt the same way toward their wives after they saw the massacre of her nether region.

Usually, and with varying degrees of success, endorphins kick in after childbirth, a kind of natural morphine produced by the central nervous system and pituitary gland that help a new mother soon forget the pain of labor and childbirth.

I think ninety-nine-point-nine percent of women would agree that once they hold their newborn baby in their arms, they would gladly go through it all again, eventually. So it can't be all that bad.

My intention with starting off with the gory bit is to help make sure you know what you're getting yourself into before you consider casually having unprotected sex with a young man or teenage boy.

When you find the right partner, I highly recommend it, because your dad and Yaca have brought me my greatest joys and were worth every varicose vein, hemorrhoid and labor pain.

If your doctor recommends iron supplements, make sure it's a brand that doesn't make you constipated. They make them now. That may be the most important and helpful advice I or anyone else will ever give you.

Your dad's birth was the worst. They didn't have epidurals in Portwey Hospital, England back then and forceps, tearing and cutting were involved.

Your dad became stuck in the birth canal, hence the forceps intervention.

You don't know pain until a doctor has fumbled around your ladies' toilet parts seemingly up to his elbows trying to find your baby's head to pull it out. And then, having taken what felt like a week to locate the head, obliged the student doctors who were observing the procedure by taking the forceps out and starting again so they could get a better view. Then, if you can believe such cruelty, taking the forceps out again and offering one student doctor the chance to have a go at clamping them on your dad's head.

Two years later, when the greatest discovery the world has ever known — epidurals — were available in our little seaside town, Yaca's birth was a positive delight. This miracle drug is injected into your spine and deadens any pain from the waist down.

There have been a few rare cases of permanent damage caused by the epidural, as well as shivering from low blood pressure and headaches during labor, but those are risks I was prepared to take and would strongly urge you to do the same.

Knowing your dad suffered breathing problems when he was born and was in intensive care for ten days due to my fear of pooing myself, I pushed Yaca out with all my might, even though you can't feel when to push, thanks to the most excellent numbing powers of the epidural.

The vast majority of those 275,000 annual maternal deaths I mentioned earlier happen in poorer countries than yours and are largely due to infection because of poor cleanliness, bad diet and untreated sexually transmitted diseases like chlamydia.

At the beginning of this millennium, the World Health Organization reported that 500,000 girls and women died during or after childbirth, so things are improving, as the figure has almost halved. Have those numbers handy when a man says childbirth is like shelling peas and women give birth in the rice fields of India, put their baby in a sling and go back to work.

On average, five Fijian women a year die during childbirth or shortly thereafter. Not bad odds, I suppose, when you consider there are around 20,000 births a year there. I do not want you to be one of those statistics. I hope I will be around to make sure you get the very best medical care should you need it when you have your first baby. I will arrange for an anesthesiologist to be flown in with a suitcase full of the best pain-relieving drugs known to woman.

Your mum had a natural childbirth when she had you. She had no other choice. Your dad and your mom's mom sat for seventy-two hours on a bench outside the hospital where you were born, while your mom was in labor. No pain-killing drugs (there weren't any available even if she wanted them) or loved one to hold her hand. The nurses wouldn't allow your dad or Nau in the delivery room. That should be a crime in my book.

An advantage of not having any pain-killing drugs during labor is that the babies are born fully alert, not drowsy. Given the option, my recommendation is to get the baby out as quickly and painlessly as possible.

I have been present at two other births as well as my own babies. Well, one birth and one very long labor.

It wasn't until the last minute that I was allowed in the delivery room when GAJ had Marley. Marley's dad is an acupuncturist and nutritionist who was pushing for a natural birth. GAJ was concerned I might punch him if he urged her not to go the epidural route while she was in labor and if the pain was getting too much.

By the time I arrived at the hospital, the epidural was working its magic and I was invited to stay for the birth. It was the most amazing and wonderful experience of my life to see Marley born.

She just popped out after three or four pushes and we were all overjoyed. GAJ never looked more beautiful. I did a good job of photographing the event, capturing the highlights while allowing GAJ to keep her dignity. No shots of the war zone.

If you are ever called upon to photograph a birth, be sure and get a shot of the clock (there's always a clock) so there's never any doubt about the time the baby was born.

I was one of about ten women who were with my friend CJ during her sixty-hour home labor. Yes, I just said sixty hours.

The plan was for her baby to come into this world by way of a birthing pool at home. Best to remember that plans have a habit of not turning out how you want. So be prepared for any eventuality and have a Plan B, C and D up your sleeve.

Those first fifty-five hours were incredible to witness. CJ had no pain-killers and was completely in control. She walked around during contractions or got in the warm water until they passed. She even went for a walk down to the beach at one point, calm and serene. She is a yoga teacher, though.

Then CJ announced calmly to the midwife that there was no way this baby was coming out naturally.

I had two jobs: to drive CJ to the hospital in case of emergency, and feed all of her friends and supporters who came and went.

Thinking the labor would only last about twelve hours, I hadn't bought enough food, and didn't have a route mapped out to get to the hospital. So I was driving while a friend talked me through the route over the phone. This was in the days when you were still allowed to talk on the cell phone while driving and before I had GPS. In the back seat, CJ was audibly praying.

Only CJ's mother was allowed in the operating room with her during the caesarian delivery. CJ's husband was away on business in another country, but had watched most of the labor via Skype until he fell asleep, exhausted, after about forty-six hours. Her mother and I were the only ones to stay the course.

CJ had a horrible reaction to the anesthetic. She was delirious and violently sick. And the recovery time is longer with a caesarian. Maybe I'm a wimp, but the important thing is for you to have the birth you want. This is the only time you will ever hear me encourage you to take drugs. Lots of them.

Many women in America choose to have a caesarian birth to avoid pelvic floor issues later. Some even opt to have a surrogate carry their baby for them. Those who choose the surrogate route usually do so as a last resort, because they have fertility problems and have tried all sorts of prodding, probing and potions to help them conceive first.

For most women, it's a primal desire to procreate. Originally, it was to ensure the survival of the species. Now women are choosing not to have children at all. How amazing to have that option.

Before contraception, women didn't have any say in the matter and had so many babies they were sick and exhausted all the time. I always wanted a family. There have been bumps in the road, but I cannot imagine life without you, your dad and Yaca. Actually, yes, I can. It would be terrible and not worth living.

Life Lesson # 5   *Never say never to painkilling drugs during childbirth.*

8

LOVE AND MARRIAGE

I've been married twice: to Grandpa and Grand Poppa C. I married Grandpa when I was just nineteen years old, which is way too young for anyone to get married. But in those days, and in the provincial seaside town where we lived, it wasn't considered acceptable for people to live together – certainly not by my parents.

I have no regrets about marrying Grandpa, because I wouldn't have your dad and Yaca if I hadn't. And we both learned from the mistakes we made as a couple to the benefit of Grand Poppa C and Grandma who we later married.

I suspect Grandpa is more communicative with and appreciative of Grandma than he was with me. And I am certainly not such a nag with Grand Poppa C as I was with Grandpa. Grand Poppa C may dispute that, but he doesn't know just how bad I was before.

Most relationships fail because at least one of the people involved doesn't feel appreciated by the other. I think that was true in my case.

I was a full-time stay-at-home mum and think I was pretty good at it. As trained by my own mother, I kept a nice home. And, though I say it myself, I was quite attractive and trim. So it pained and frustrated me that Grandpa seemed to prefer being in the pub than with me, once your dad and Yaca were in bed.

By the time I had been married to Grandpa for nine years, my life was one long round of nappies (diapers), cooking and cleaning. GAJ was a backing singer for British pop star Mari Wilson. I went to one of the gigs, in Exeter, and locked eyes with the bass player, Colin.

My heart was all a-flutter. His, too, apparently. We met again a few months later at a Mari concert at the London Palladium and progressed to full-on flirtation, followed by a few months of letter writing.

Colin told me I was beautiful (no one else ever had) and I felt cherished and adored by him. When we met up again a couple of months later in London and made love for the first time, he awakened something inside me that had been long dead.

I wasn't so stupid as to leave Grandpa and break up our family just for another man. I left Grandpa because I knew I didn't want to spend the rest of my life with someone who didn't appreciate me.

Colin was certainly a catalyst and even if I wouldn't have left Grandpa at that time, we would have broken up eventually. Colin made it clear he wasn't in a position to set up home with me and my kids in Weymouth, Dorset, as he was a musician who needed to be in London. But he would come and visit me whenever he could.

The break-up with Grandpa was horrible and painful. Your dad and Yaca, aged four and two at the time, and Grandpa, were deeply upset about it.

I'm not recommending breaking up a family, but Grandpa and I have found happiness with our new spouses who are both much more suitable partners for us.

Grandpa met Grandma within a year of our break-up and they had a son of their own, Elliott. One of the things I am most grateful for in life is that Grandma has always been a loving and consistent presence in the lives of your dad and Yaca.

Colin and I didn't fare so well. We lasted about eighteen months. He was away on tour for most of the time. When he did come to stay with us, your dad and Yaca didn't make him feel welcome. We were broke and living miles apart. What little money Colin earned as a musician was spent on petrol (gas) to come and see me.

I was never a gold-digger, but would have liked a boyfriend who could at least afford to buy me a cup of tea. The relationship went downhill when I suggested Colin might like to consider getting a proper job.

Colin said, "I have a job. I'm a guitar player." I may have rolled my eyes. He had switched from bass to guitar by now and, while there were a few great gigs and TV appearances, it was mostly a financial struggle.

He got a regular gig playing guitar in a trio at a pizza restaurant in London for about £30 a night, twice a week. His trips to see me became even less frequent. Why would I want to be with a guy who would rather play guitar in a pizza restaurant for not much money than be with me? So we broke up.

Don't worry, I was rarely lonely. I usually had a gentleman caller on the go. What can I tell you? I was popular. I didn't marry again, but I had a few proposals and was a serial monogamist (which means I was faithful to whomever I was dating at the time). Those relationships usually lasted about two years and a pattern formed. Not ideal, but it worked. For me.

We moved to London from Weymouth (with Grandpa's blessing) when your dad and Yaca were sixteen and fourteen. Your dad won a place at the Brits School of the Performing Arts in Croydon and thrived. Yaca didn't want to go and was miserable for three years until she moved back to Weymouth to live with Grandpa, Grandma and Elliott.

Your dad graduated from the Brits School and set up his own record label. He left home on the Tuesday and I moved to Los Angeles on the Thursday to live with GAJ for a year. It's a real end of an era when your kids leave home and I was concerned I might go mad with Empty Nest Syndrome if I didn't embark on a new adventure.

I loved LA and never moved back to England. Your dad and Yaca came to stay a couple of times a year and I went back home regularly to see them and my parents.

I had a very nice gentlemen caller (of course I did), as did GAJ, and life was sweet until GAJ went and ruined our perfect setup by deciding to make a new home and start a family of her own with Arthur.

My gentlemen caller and I didn't want to move forward in our relationship, so we broke up. My book, *Plus One: A Year in the Life of a Hollywood Nobody,* was being published the following year (publishing is a slow business), I was technically homeless and more than a little anxious about my future. I went back to England for three months to re-group and make a plan for the next phase of my life.

One of my top mates is Sue Turton, who I met when we were both working shifts at Independent Television News in London. She went on to become an award-winning reporter for Channel 4 News and was also a regular visitor to LA to see me. On this occasion, Sue suggested we go to Prague for the weekend.

There's a terrific book about marriage called *Committed*, by Elizabeth Gilbert. She explores the history of and compromise required for marriage. Ms. Gilbert mentions a therapist friend of hers who said her female clients could be separated into two groups: those who are married and wish they weren't and those who aren't and wish they were.

As we sipped our cappuccinos in Wenceslas Square, Sue said she would swap her two Royal Television Society Awards, her great job that took her around the world at a moment's notice and her house in the country to find Mr. Right and have a couple of kids.

I asked her if she had ever met a guy who she thought might have been "the one" but it hadn't worked out at the time. There was one guy. Sometimes the timing is wrong.

"How about you? Who was the love of your life?" said Sue.

"Colin," I said. "It was twenty years ago. I had two young kids, we were broke and we lived three hours' drive apart."

At that precise moment, my cell phone rang. It was Colin.

I had sent out an email blast before I left LA giving my UK cell number to my British pals. A few years back, when our friend Jenny died aged forty from cancer, leaving three young kids, GAJ and I had one of our philosophical conversations where we checked whether we were satisfied with our lives – just in case we, too, died young. We both felt we had followed the right paths and had no regrets.

But I decided I would want two former boyfriends, Colin and one other, to know they had been significant in my life and that I was grateful for their love, even though it hadn't worked out between us.

I tracked them both down via mutual friends and emailed them saying just that and making it clear I was in no way trying to rekindle our relationship, which I wasn't. I did not make a habit to look back with regret or reconnect with old flames.

Their email addresses must have been added to my contacts list automatically. While I was stunned that Colin had called right at the time I had said out loud that he had been the love of my life, I did not want to see him again. I said I would call him when I got back to London. I didn't.

He called me the day before my return to LA and invited me out to dinner. I told him it was my last night, another time maybe. I knew he had a day job by now as a car journalist and played guitar in a covers band at night, and rather hoped he would be busy. But he wasn't.

Colin picked me up in a turbocharged sports sedan, a Mitsubishi Evo VIII in red with a ridiculous rear wing. A tad flash for my taste, but it was a press car he had to review for BBC *Top Gear Magazine*.

He drove me to The Red Pepper in Maida Vale. I stole a glance. He looked well. Handsome, even.

The waiter handed us menus. Colin looked at me over his menu and said, "I love you. I've always loved you. I have a job, a house, I do yoga and I'm not a jerk any more. How do you feel about getting back together?"

I explained that I was not in the market for a casual fling. In fact,

I wasn't looking for a relationship at all. Even if I was, he would have to woo me.

"Fair enough," he said.

We spent the next twenty-four hours together. Our love-making was as wonderful as I remembered. I wouldn't recommend sleeping with anyone so soon, but we did have a history and I had to make sure there was still chemistry before I went back to LA.

"You're a wonderful lover," I said.

"You're a wonder to love."

"How come you've never married?" I said.

"Other women are like weak tea compared to you."

Good answers.

He had kept all my love letters from twenty years before. We found them in a cardboard box tied up with red ribbon in one of the spare bedrooms in his huge house.

"I expect you've got all your old girlfriends' letters here somewhere," I said, fishing.

"No other letters. Or cards."

Jolly good. And no children. The house was rented, though. Swings and roundabouts.

I had kept his love letters too. They were in a box in my parents' attic.

It was a blissful time. Only one hiccup, about who's best: The Beatles or The Beach Boys?

Ridiculous. The Beatles are way better. But it didn't seem worth breaking up over, and so soon into the relationship. He drove me to the airport.

I walked into my temporary new home in LA and the phone was ringing.

"Hello?" I said.

"Woooooood. Wooooooooooo. Woooooooooooooooo," said the ghostly voice on the other end of the phone.

"Who is this?"

"You said I had to woo you," said Colin.

We spoke several times a day for a month.

"Will you come back to England for another visit soon?" he said.

"I can't afford the plane fare. I should really get a job," I said. "My book isn't due out for another year."

"I'll pay for your ticket and your expenses so you don't have to get a job," he said.

Remember what I said about being financially independent? Sometimes you have to compromise.

So I went back to England for two weeks. Which turned into three, then four.

Time to tell your dad and Yaca. They remembered him. Even though they were only five and three at the time when we broke up and twenty years had passed.

"Wasn't he the ginger?" said your dad. He said "ginger" to rhyme with ringer.

"What hair he has left does have a strawberry hue, yes." I said.

"So long as you're happy, mum," said Yaca none too convincingly.

The four of us went out for a curry up the road from your dad's apartment in West Hampstead. I was nervous, but it went well. Your dad and Yaca were amazing: funny, intelligent and charming. Phew.

Colin suggested they make a note of his phone number. Your dad punched the numbers into his cell phone and listed Colin as "The Home Wrecker." I laughed nervously as your dad said "The Home Wrecker" again in case we missed it the first time.

Yaca turned her phone to calculator mode. "Twenty years' pocket money at fifteen pounds a month equals three thousand six hundred pounds. I'll take a check."

Up until this point, I had always paid for your dad and Yaca's plane fares to come to LA. It wasn't their fault that their mother lived an ocean away, so it didn't seem right they should use their hard-earned cash to come to see me. They had little to spare anyway.

This was going to be the first Christmas we were going to be apart as my credit cards were maxed out. Colin sold two of his guitars to pay for their tickets. I didn't ask him to. He just did it.

We had a fantastic Christmas. Unbeknown to me, Colin asked your dad and Yaca for their blessing to propose to me. They gave it unreservedly.

Colin proposed the following March, on my fiftieth birthday. He gave up the job that made him so attractive this time around and sold some more of his guitars to fund his move to LA. Given the choice, we both preferred to live in LA.

We married fourteen months later. My dad and your dad walked me down the steps to our waiting friends and family, and Yaca was my beautiful bridesmaid. GAJ was best lady man and both my and Colin's parents were there.

In his wedding speech, Colin thanked our parents for living long enough to see us get married. He also promised me he'd love and cherish me forever and be funny, but not as funny as me. As if.

Grand Poppa C, as you know him, has been true to his word and not a day has gone by when I haven't felt loved and cherished by him. We have faced enormous challenges during our ten years together (this time around), much more serious than the Beatles/Beach Boys dilemma.

He quickly established himself as a freelance car journalist of note and wrote for many prestigious publications, including the *Los Angeles Times* and *European Car* magazine among others. Of course, he was happiest playing guitar and was soon playing for several girl singers, including GAJ.

Within six months of our wedding, your dad moved from London to LA to live with us while he planned the next phase of his life and slept on our couch. That was actually a fun time. I had both of them playing guitar and laughing at *South Park* and *Family Guy*. They found fart gags to be especially hilarious.

When Yaca came to visit and one child was on the couch and the other on a blow-up bed, I felt shame that we couldn't afford a two- or three-bedroom place so my kids could have a bed each when they came to see me. But they convinced me they didn't care and the important thing was that we were together.

I finally had the happy family I had always craved.

Your dad went to Fiji and settled there. Yaca had her dream job in TV comedy. Grand Poppa C had a horrible daily commute to a car magazine where he worked as a copy editor and feature writer, but we were all happy.

Life was perfect. Grand Poppa C would go to work. I'd play

tennis or go to a yoga class in the mornings, meet a friend for lunch, write for four hours then cook dinner over which Grand Poppa C and I would catch up on our day.

We needed a second car, though, as Grand Poppa C couldn't guarantee he'd have a press car to use. He wanted to buy an old second-hand car, but I convinced him we should lease a new one. Which we did.

I also convinced him, against his better judgment, that he was irreplaceable at the car magazine and should demand a pay rise. Not only did Grand Poppa C not get a pay rise, he was laid off. And before the first car payment was due.

The next couple of years were difficult. We had nothing to discuss over dinner. Neither of us had much work.

I said, "I'll get a full-time job."

"Any idea when that might be?"

I needed to get out of the apartment anyway. Grand Poppa C constantly in my creative space was not conducive to my writing. There was also a danger that I might kill him if he didn't stop doing his daily guitar scales and arpeggios along to a metronome.

I became even more of a nag and he withdrew even more into his shell. Grand Poppa C wasn't chatty at the best of times. He took so long to answer friends' questions that I started answering for him.

Not emptying the overflowing trash without being asked became the final straw. The quieter he got, the angrier I became. GAJ suggested couples therapy.

We learned we had to compromise. Meet each other half way. I had to stop answering for him, however long it took. He had to voice his feelings more. Turns out he was scared of me. Can you believe that? The therapist was surprised I hadn't been more compassionate that Colin had lost his job. What was the source of my anger, she wondered? Moving swiftly on, I prefer to consider myself passionate and colorful rather than angry or shouty.

Crucially, we had to start communicating better and actually listen to each other to such a degree that we each had to repeat what the other just said to show we were really listening.

The ice was broken during a therapy session when Grand Poppa C was describing something I had said and the therapist asked how that had made him feel.

"I thought she was being a complete cow," he said.

The therapist flinched in shock that he had called me such a terrible name. "How did it make you feel, Claire, when Colin just called you a cow?"

This was too much for me and I started laughing. "It didn't bother me at all," I said in all honesty.

I've called him a stupid bastard before for putting too much milk in my tea.

Grand Poppa C said that he wished I was more supportive of his guitar playing. He said he felt I resented his playing when, next to me, music is his greatest love and he was getting paid gigs from it.

The therapist asked him if his parents had praised his playing when he was young. They never did. That was heartbreaking to me, as he is brilliant.

My beef with him was that he was so bloody quiet, especially in company.

"Why do you think you are so quiet, Colin?" asked the therapist.

"I can't imagine that anyone would ever be interested in anything I have to say."

"You're the smartest and most talented man I have ever met!" I shrieked.

Then we fell into each other's arms and have never looked back.

Five years on from therapy, we both still work mostly from home and are together twenty-four-seven. He checks my work and I check his. I go to most of his gigs and cheer the loudest after his amazing solos. There's plenty to talk about over dinner. I wash up. He dries.   Then we settle down to watch some TV, preferably a comedy. I sit at one end of the couch. He sits at the other and he holds my feet. All evening. Tenderly and lovingly. The way Grand Poppa C holds my feet makes my heart melt.

When I see the trash can is almost full I say in a kindly voice, "Love, would you be so kind as to empty the trash?"

"I think what you are saying, Claire, is that the trash is almost full and needs emptying. It will be my honor and my pleasure to do that small task for you. For us." We laugh a lot.

Grand Poppa C still practices guitar. You have to if you want to stay good at anything. The metronome is packed away. Compromise, you see.

Married life has been made sweeter with the discovery of "The World's Finest Natural Ear Plugs" that keep out snoring and other noises, particularly bathroom sounds. Those ear plugs help us keep the mystery alive in our tiny apartment.

We have designated certain areas of responsibility. I am head of cooking and most of the cleaning. Grand Poppa C is too slow for my liking, so I might as well do it myself. He is in charge of computers, cars, spiders and clearing cobwebs on the veranda. We are a good team. We take a walk most afternoons, or play tennis. I don't want him to die prematurely from a heart attack. I'm in this for the long haul. I'm not completely stupid.

The reason I have shared this deeply personal stuff is to show you that relationships need to be worked at.

Life Lesson # 6   *A good marriage needs chemistry, communication and commitment. And some love glue.*

Recommended further reading: *Getting The Love You Want* by Harville Hendrix, *Men are from Mars, Women are from Venus* by John Gray.

9

WRITING

Whatever you do in life, to do it well, you need to be able to read and write.

I started out as a journalist in England writing for my local evening newspaper, then progressed to television news before moving to LA after your dad and Yaca left home, at which point I joined the hoards of others attempting to make it as a writer in Tinseltown.

I soon learned that it is almost impossible to make a reasonable living as a writer, artist, actor, singer or musician.

In an ideal world, to make sure you don't lose your mind trying to earn a crust solely as a creative, you need a trust fund, a wealthy spouse or a big lottery win. You'll need something to keep you going before you write that best-selling book or hit song.

While I am the last person who wants to crush your creative spirit, I am here to tell you that the vast majority of artists need another source of income and an ability to take a metaphorical punch to the gut many times and still keep getting up. Chances are your work will be rejected and criticized over and over again before you make a sale. But don't let me stop you. If you want to be a writer or singer, you have to believe you will be the next JK Rowling or Beyoncé.

Here's the thing: if you do have a creative calling and don't pursue it, you might die of misery or boredom. And that will never do.

Do what you love and love what you do. You'll be unfulfilled if you don't. You'll feel in the pit of your stomach that something big is missing from your life and you might not even realize what it is. If you ever do feel that way, pause for a moment and wonder if you might be doing a job that you positively hate and isn't feeding your creative soul.

The best advice I can give if you do choose a creative path is to follow it because you love doing it and not because you think it will make any money. If you do make money from it, consider that an added bonus.

Think about what you want to do and stay focused on it. Practice your craft. People who succeed at anything work really hard at it. The best musicians and artists practice every day, sometimes for eight hours at a time, until they get good at it — longer if they want to be great at it. And then they have to keep practicing to stay great.

If you want to be a writer, write something every day. If you can't think of anything to write about, read. Learn from the best. Be inspired. Keep busy. Find your tribe. Surround yourself with like-minded people who inspire you and share your values. Avoid the naysayers and mean-spirited.

Once you've made your mind up to be, say, a writer and until you sell something, you will probably have to take a, gulp, job. Ideally something you like or are good at.

The people you work with might even be a source of inspiration and you might make a good friend.

Keep your monthly financial outgoings down to a minimum. Live simply. The best and most successful artists have waited tables, tended bars or cleaned other peoples' toilets at some time or another.

Don't get me started on the music business. You just have to keep going to have any chance of even a taste of success and know that it might be fleeting.

I have had some terrific temporary jobs in between writing projects working as a TV producer and on films. I have usually been the oldest person on the set and sometimes done some menial tasks but at least I'm still in the game.

It wasn't much fun being an assistant to a physical therapist. It may have been the timing, coming a year after my book, *Plus One: A Year In The Life Of A Hollywood Nobody*, was published and it wasn't the big hit I'd hoped and dreamed. Not that I thought it was brilliant, but it was good enough and I had read *The Secret*. As instructed by *The Secret* author Rhonda Byrne, I asked, believed and waited for it to be a financial success that spawned a movie and sequel. I am still waiting.

It wasn't that I was too proud to be someone's assistant and I pride myself that I did a good job, but Grand Poppa C and I had just watched an episode of *Weeds* and the main character was applying for a job as an assistant. She made it clear during the interview that she wouldn't scoop, sweep or fold. And I had to do all those things in my job.

I felt very sorry for myself. It didn't help that my boss's wife was writing a book and was able to do it because he paid the bills.

Be careful what you wish for, because I started thinking his wife could do what I was doing as she sure as hell wasn't spending much time writing. He thought so too and I was made redundant. I console myself that the experience was character building.

In the meantime, my literary agent had rejected several of my next brilliant book proposals. So I still needed to earn some money to help keep a roof over our head and food in our bellies. Grand Poppa C was doing pretty well writing about cars and playing guitar yet it wasn't enough to keep us both going. I started looking for other jobs but there weren't any going that were as good as the one I'd talked myself out of.

That was a challenging time. There wasn't a job offered for 55-year-old women with excellent life skills and a great sense of humor. Most of the jobs advertised on places like Craigslist wanted young and enthusiastic assistants with college degrees.

One job offer in particular had me laughing and crying at the same time. The employer was looking for a "part-time" assistant to work four days a week from seven in the morning until seven in the evening caring for her three young children and running errands. Only applicants with a degree (no actors) need apply and they had to be familiar with fine dining. The pay was $12 an hour. As if that wasn't bad enough, applicants had to submit a handwritten letter explaining all about themselves, their star sign and where they wanted to be in five years.

Not working for you, crazy lady.

Accepting that it was not an advantage to be in my mid-fifties and looking for a job, I thought long and hard about what I liked and what I was good at. I'm a good cook, but catering is a thankless task and, with the possible exception of coal mining, the hardest job with the longest hours. I'd done a few catering gigs, but didn't enjoy dealing with people who quibbled over every cent and who were usually impossible to please.

I like most children and they often like me, so I babysit. I'm practically perfect at it in every way.

Grand Poppa C, by the way, is miserable when he isn't doing

regular gigs playing guitar. He was a full-time professional musician for twenty years before he started writing about cars to supplement his income.

Not that we have so many choices at our age, but we have made a conscious decision to live creative lives knowing there may be lean patches where we have to supplement our incomes.

Steven Pressfield summed it up perfectly in his book, *The War of Art: Break Through the Blocks & Win Your Inner Creative Battles:* "The artist committing himself to his calling has volunteered for hell, whether he knows it or not. He will be dining for the duration on a diet of isolation, rejection, self-doubt, despair, ridicule, contempt, and humiliation."

The premise of Pressfield's book is that resistance is a creative person's tireless and impersonal nemesis, and you have to resign yourself to battle it. You will encounter the worst and most heartbreaking obstacles around that which you are most called to do. It defines the different forms resistance takes and recommends that an artist hunker down and assumes the mentality of a professional soldier in an endless conflict.

Most people who achieve success would agree that luck plays a part. Maybe they were in the right place at the right time, or knew someone who knew someone who could help or guide them. Yes, it's a battle at times, but the harder we work, the luckier we are. And the ones who make it are the ones who don't give up.

By the way, there are many ways to be creative without trying to make a living at it. Gardening, cooking, sewing, knitting, playing an instrument, painting, singing, and writing for the sheer pleasure of doing it and completing a project is a wonderful thing, and also feeds the soul.

Even if you don't want to be a professional writer, it's still important that your writing be grammatically correct and punctuated properly. Whether it's a letter, email or a job application you're writing, do it right.

An employer friend once told me she doesn't even bother to interview applicants who can't spell or punctuate. It's harder for some people to spell than others. Even dyslexia (problems with reading and writing sometimes known as word blindness) can be overcome with practice and patience.

Here are some common speech and grammatical errors that it is my fervent hope no man, woman or child sharing my DNA will ever commit. But they do.

The plural of a word is denoted by adding an s not 's. It's CDs, books, DVDs, dogs, etc. Not CD's, book's, DVD's or dog's. The correct use of an apostrophe denotes belonging to as in a CD's cover or a book's title or a dog's breakfast. "It's" is an abbreviation of "it is" or "it has."

This is guaranteed to get my eye twitching when I hear or see it: it's should've/could've/would've — not should of/could of/would of. To be on the safe side, best write it in full: should have/could have/would have.

I'm not a fan of the semi-colon (;) either. There's rarely a situation where a comma won't do instead. Frankly, I think they're a bit pretentious, as are "whom" and "whilst."

Grand Poppa C, who also works as a copy editor, can't abide exclamation marks. He says it's the literary equivalent of laughing at your own joke. Guilty as charged!

Unless you are Irish or born in the north of England, where it is common usage (but still wrong), the letter "H" is pronounced and spelled "aitch" not "haitch."

"You're" is an abbreviation of "you are" not anything to do with "your."

Never be smug about your grammatical skills and judge others too harshly, because we all make mistakes. I only learned recently that I have been guilty of a classic error in asking for a slither of cake. Snakes slither. It's a sliver of cake.

Most people have several different careers during their lifetime and there's nothing wrong with deciding something isn't for you after all. Just be sure that you are stopping being a "whatever" because you want to, not because your parents or grandparents suggested it was time.

When I said "whatever" in the previous paragraph, it was to denote "the creative pursuit of your choice" and not said in the whiney, irritating tone of a teenage girl suffering from surly cow syndrome.

Another pet hate of mine is when anyone over the age of eight calls their parents Mummy and Daddy. Finally, if you've said or written something you consider amusing, it is not necessary to add LOL *(exclamation mark that was here removed by Grand Poppa C. He let the others slide)*.

So, my darling, I don't know what you will do for a living when you grow up, but I hope you feel the joy of being paid to do something you love. And experience the relief of getting paid for writing a book, article or song every now and then so you can look the metaphorical wolf in the eye as he circles your door and say, "Not this time, sunshine."

Life Lesson # 7 Work is hard. That's why it's called work. So best work at something you love.

Recommended further reading: *Eats, Shoots & Leaves: The Zero Tolerance Approach to Punctuation* by Lynne Truss, *On Writing: A Memoir of the Craft* by Stephen King, *Story* by Robert McKee, *The Artist's Way* by Julia Cameron. *The War of Art: Break Through the Blocks & Win Your Inner Creative Battles* by Steven Pressfield and *Bird by Bird* by Anne Lamott.

10

CLAIREY POPPINS

A movie, *The Making Of Plus One*, (inspired by my book) had been premiered at the Cannes film festival and I had the most wonderful time there. My literary agent was shopping my latest book proposal to publishers, I had found a fabulous producing partner for my TV reality show and we were pitching the idea to production companies. I was getting paid, sometimes, to write articles for national newspapers and magazines.

You could have been forgiven for thinking I was doing rather well. However, I don't know if you've heard, but there was a bit of a recession going on in the early 2000s, so freelance writers like me weren't exactly raking in the cash.

The first time I looked after then five-year-old Marzhan, she asked me if I had ever seen *Mary Poppins* and would I like to watch it with her? Oh yes. I had absolute joy in my heart as we sang along to all the songs at the tops of our voices.

Marzhan asked me to sing to her and rub her back like her mum does when she tucks her into bed. I sang as much as I could remember of "Feed The Birds, Tuppence a Bag" while I rubbed her back.

She said, "I love you, Clairey Poppins."

I said, "I love you, Marzhan." And I really do. The name Clairey Poppins kinda stuck.

I still have play dates with Marzhan, but for love not money and because I want to, not because I have to. When you take action to improve your circumstances, there are often unexpected and life-affirming consequences, like my relationship with Marzhan.

I had two other occasional charges – siblings Prakesh and Mangala. Before I tell you about those two slices of perfection, please know how hard it is for me having so many Ms in my life: my daughter, my son, two nieces, Muttley the dog, my brother Mark (known as GUM since your birth, short for Great Uncle Mark), two of the little girls I looked after and now you. I don't call any of them by the right name first time and have been known to go through the entire list of Ms before I get it right. I will never judge my parents again for calling their children by the wrong name. Please grant me and other senior citizens the same courtesy.

I vowed to be the best darned babysitter ever until one of my creative projects hit the jackpot. And frankly, I was. I happily and energetically played Teen Titans with Mangala and Prakesh.

Prakesh was Beast Boy, Mangala was Starfire and I got to be

Raven, who can lift really heavy things. Prakesh ran around shouting, "I am not a man. I am an animal." I ran around flexing my, erm, muscles.

Once Prakesh and Mangala had grown bored with that, they showed me the family photo taken at their uncle's wedding. They painstakingly went through everyone, explaining who they were, how old, how nice, etc. I asked if they saw much of their mum's family.

Mangala, aged four, said, "Our mom's dad, Big Papa, died young. He ate hamburgers. You shouldn't eat cow if you want to live a long time." Mangala skipped off and came back carrying a heavy box wrapped in green velvet.

"This is Big Papa. He was cremated. His tiny crushed-up bits of bone and stuff are in this box," she said.

Prakesh, aged six, said, "Big Papa may be in heaven, but he'll forever be in our hearts."

It felt like a change of scene would be a good idea, so I suggested a swim in the communal pool. There was a "No Running" sign by the pool, but Prakesh and Mangala, like all children, preferred to dive or jump in, get out, run round to the other side and dive or jump in again. Fearing they might break a limb on my watch and wondering why they kept ignoring my polite requests to slow down, I asked them in my best Mary Poppins voice, "Now children, what's the number-one swimming pool rule?"

Prakesh replied confidently, "No farting."

As Stan Marsh said on *South Park*, "It's all about moderation. If you never fart, you combust. But if you always fart, you deplete the ozone. So we must fart only at the appropriate time or when it's really, really funny."

Experience has taught me that I am absolutely brilliant with children for four hours at a time and then my patience starts to wear a bit thin.

Life Lesson # 8 *Even if you don't get to have children of your own, you can still love them, be loved back by one or two if you're lucky and have a positive influence on other young lives.*

11

THE DEMON DRINK

Grand Poppa C and I were listening to *This American Life* on NPR. The segment was about people who regularly eat certain foods despite being severely allergic to them.

The reporter described an otherwise intelligent colleague who came to work with a face so swollen and deformed he was unrecognizable. "The Elephant Man" told his concerned and traumatized co-workers not to worry as he had eaten seafood to which he was severely allergic but he loved it so much he ate it once a month anyway.

The segment gave other examples of people who were prepared to have their stomach pumped and go to hospital for emergency shots to bring them back from the brink of death on a regular basis because they like wheat, dairy or even strawberries so much they couldn't live without them.

I turned to Grand Poppa C and said, "Stupid, stupid bastards." And I judged them for days, muttering under my breath "stupid,

stupid bastards" whenever I thought of them. This lasted for weeks until I realized I was as stupid as them because I still drink alcohol. Maybe twice a week (more over the Christmas season) and yet it makes me feel like varying degrees of utter shit. From slightly wooly headed to a head-pounding, pure puking hell when I have vowed never to touch another drop. But I do.

Probably ninety-five percent of all headaches I've ever had have been because I drank alcohol. Most sleepless nights are due to drinking that extra glass of wine that plays havoc with your sleep patterns.

And I don't even drink that much. I should stick to one glass of wine, but it's usually two and occasionally three — never more than half a bottle of wine. Well, occasionally more than half a bottle of wine, when I am guaranteed to feel absolutely dreadful.

Every argument I have ever started with a husband, boyfriend, family member, or friend has been when I've been drinking alcohol. If both of us have been drinking, it can get really ugly and upsetting.

Compared to many people I know, I hardly drink at all. Your dad and Yaca call me the alcohol police because I can't stand being around drunk people.

I usually stop drinking after a maximum of three glasses, even when I know I should stop at one. So while I may get a bit loud (louder) and not as funny as I think I am at the time, I don't get stupid, violent or belligerent (well, maybe belligerent seven times tops in my entire life), I judge people who do uncompromisingly.

There will come a time when I shall stop drinking completely and it will probably be because I want to lose weight (alcohol is just empty calories) and the pleasure I get from a glass of fine wine with a good meal or during a romantic or interesting conversation will not be worth the headache I know will come with it. I'm surprised it's taking me so long to reach the obvious conclusion that I'd have more money, be slimmer and feel much better if I didn't drink at all.

Even if I don't feel dreadful the morning after, I never feel great. I don't drink spirits (which are poison to me) and only occasionally a beer if I'm eating curry.

There's a lot to be said for never drinking alcohol at all, thereby avoiding the aforementioned hangovers and arguments. Let's not forget, a decent bottle of wine to share with a friend is not cheap.

Some people should stop drinking completely because alcohol can and does ruin lives. If you ever get to the stage where you have lost a job, home, husband or friendship because you are repeatedly drunk, it's time to stop altogether. It will be hard, but it can be done.

As with all indigenous populations like Native Americans, Aborigines and Maoris, Fijians have a lower tolerance to alcohol than the colonial forces (white men) who introduced it to their countries. Almost all crime is related to drugs or alcohol.

Here's a sobering fact: the vast majority of unplanned pregnancies happen when at least one of the two people involved have had too much to drink.

I am what's called a moderate drinker. Most heavy drinkers (and smokers) stop drinking because their doctors tell them they will die if they don't. Or their lives have become unmanageable. Whatever the reason, they need to stop hanging with their drinking buddies and make some big, seemingly overwhelming and unbearable changes before they can become happy and healthy.

Don't worry, if you are ever unlucky enough to be addicted to drugs or alcohol, I know some amazing people who can help you.

Neither of my parents were big drinkers. In fact, I don't recall them drinking at all when I was a kid, maybe a glass of sherry at Christmas.

Funnily enough, they started drinking more in their seventies, when they would crack open a bottle of wine if the sun came out to celebrate the good weather and drink it in their English country garden, saving a glass for dinner.

I think my attraction to the idea of a cocktail hour or wine with dinner began with the TV series, *Dallas*. The wealthy Ewing family would meet every evening for cocktails before dinner. They all lived together in the same, enormous house, Southfork Ranch. I associated alcohol with wealth and success. I still aspire to having a home big enough that we could all live comfortably together.

Mind you, Grand Poppa C and I live in a one-bedroom apartment but we had you, your mum, dad and Yaca come to stay with us for two weeks and had a wonderful time. The toilet only got blocked up once.

Grand Poppa C was able to sleep at a friend's apartment just up the road. He called it his Fortress of Sanity. We all ate together at ours. You never adjusted to Pacific Time and didn't go to bed until five one morning. Mostly you were in bed by two. I confess I wasn't as patient with my children's sleeping patterns as your parents are with you.

Of course, there were desperate times when I took them out for a drive in the car to get them off to sleep if they were still awake at midnight, but your mum and dad were positively cheerful when they walked you around the marina at four in the morning.

I digress. When I left my parents' home and married Grandpa, I wanted to have a selection of spirits to offer people when they entered our home. I learned quickly that the more tempting things you keep in your home — like cake, candy, chocolate, crisps and booze — the more you'll eat and drink them.

I only buy wine and cake when Grand Poppa C and I have people coming over for dinner or if it's a birthday or anniversary.

I was going to have a whole chapter about drugs and the evil therein, but the truth is I don't know much about them as they've never appealed to me. Well, that's not strictly true. I did have a bite of a hash brownie at a dinner party when I was forty-one and was completely stoned. I didn't like that feeling at all. As you may have gathered, I like to be in control.

Then I had a puff of a joint at a party when I was forty-four that, I was warned at the time, was very strong stuff and coupled with the two glasses of wine I'd already drunk practically put me in a coma for three days after I'd puked my guts up.

If you are ever offered drugs, please just say no. Even pot can do your head in.

If you still need convincing, do an Internet search (on the laptop I've bought you for agreeing never to smoke) and look at "before" and "after" photos of drug addicts.

See what I did there? I didn't say "agreeing never to smoke cigarettes" but "never to smoke" which, as any good lawyer will tell you, includes cannabis resin, also known as marijuana.

Life Lesson # 9 *A little of what you fancy does you good. But if you can't do potentially addictive things in moderation, don't do them at all.*

Recommended listening: *This American Life* on NPR whenever possible and TED talks. Thanks to the Internet, it's always possible

12

FEELING GOOD

I can't poo and I can't sleep. There, I said it. I realize this is probably way too much information, but I want you to know that everybody has relatively mild medical "issues" that cause them varying degrees of grief, frustration, discomfort and embarrassment.

I've tried everything to cure my insomnia except prescription sleeping tablets. I even gave up caffeine for three weeks, but it didn't make any difference.

The best sleeping aid for me is one over-the-counter generic antihistamine per night taken with a little water just before bed. Don't waste your money on Benadryl. Kroger, CVS or Equaline generic antihistamines work even better and are a fifth of the price. Benadryl makes my heart race if I use it for longer than a week and that can't be good.

Grand Poppa C just told me about a study that showed people who regularly take antihistamines have a higher risk of developing

Alzheimers so don't do it for long.

I'm not on any prescription meds apart from the occasional antibiotic for bronchitis. But if I have a headache, I take one over-the-counter migraine tablet that's mostly aspirin with a splash of caffeine in it.

For muscular pain, toothache and period pain (when I had them), ibuprofen. Ibuprofen works well for rheumatic or mild arthritic pain. It's a pain killer and an anti-inflammatory.

If you can't sleep due to muscular pain, take one and a half Tylenol PM with a little water just before bed time. It's the best drug in the world. But only occasionally. It's the antihistamine in the Tylenol PM that makes you sleep like a baby.

Why do we say "sleep like a baby" as if that's the best night's sleep you'll ever have when every baby I've ever known wakes every couple of hours and takes forever to get back off?

When it comes to health, I'm a great believer in prevention being better than the cure. And although it pains me to admit it, my mother (your great-grandmother, Muriel Fordham) is right, "Everything in moderation." That was her mantra when I was growing up and it still is.

But even moderation should be used in moderation. I remember Mum once thoroughly enjoying a raw carrot. When I offered to get her another one, she said, "No, thank you. I don't want to get addicted."

Deeply suspicious of all medication, my mum rarely takes even an aspirin. When she went into labor with GAJ, it was the midwife's day off. Dad delivered the baby at home. Great Uncle Mark (GUM) and I slept soundly in our rooms throughout because Mum didn't make a sound.

This stoicism has come in handy for me in particular. Mum had such terrible morning sickness when she was expecting me that her doctor prescribed a new wonder drug, Thalidomide. She wouldn't take it. Thalidomide caused severe physical abnormalities in the children of women who took it while pregnant.

Your great-grandmother did occasionally take a course of antibiotics when she had severe bronchitis and is currently receiving vitamin B12 shots for pernicious anemia.

She never smoked. Which means she is strong and healthy and can look after my dad who did smoke and isn't nearly as fit as her.

My friend Suzanne Donovan, a professor of clinical medicine, advises against marrying a smoker as it's a given you will spend the last twenty years of your life taking care of them.

Here are some tips to improve your chances of a long and healthy life – accepting that you have been blessed with good genes and assuming you don't meet with an accident.

1. Don't smoke.

2. Eat a healthy diet which means avoiding fat and sugar, and eating organic meat and fish in moderation. Plenty of fruit and vegetables. Don't even start drinking sodas.

3. Drink plenty of water. If you get a headache, you're probably dehydrated. Drink a glass of water before popping a pain killer. Most people don't drink enough water.

4. Take regular exercise. Get moving.

5. Take a regular yoga class. At the very least, start each day with four sun salutations and hold plank position for one full minute. Time yourself. Don't trust yourself to count the seconds.

6. Meditate every day.

7. If you are putting on too much weight, eat less and exercise more.

8. Don't be obsessed with your weight.

9. If you're feeling sad, get moving. Go for a walk. If you're really fed up, put on some music and dance. Or go outside and skip down the road. I guarantee you will start smiling again.

10. Don't smoke (in case it didn't sink in the first time).

If you ever suffer from depression, which is a persistent and deep misery that can last for months, seek professional help. Depression is not the same as feeling a bit low for a couple of days. That will pass and it's OK to be sad. I've never suffered with depression having been blessed with a (mostly) happy gene. While I'm not a fan of medication unless absolutely necessary, I've witnessed a few friends (and those around them) who have benefitted enormously from taking anti-depressants for a short time when afflicted.

I'm going to assume there's a cure for cancer by the time you are sixteen. If not and I'm no longer around to help you through it, if you follow the tips above, chances are you won't get it.

If you do, know that being diagnosed with cancer isn't a death sentence. Some cancers are more deadly than others, of course, but many aren't deadly at all.

With what I know right now, if I had a cancerous lump in a breast, I'd have it removed - just the lump, not the whole breast. I have a healthy mistrust and serious doubts about the efficacy of chemotherapy. It might kill some cancer cells, but it also destroys the immune system which is nature's way of curing disease.

If you don't want to get diabetes, which is rife in Fiji, don't indulge in sugar-laden foods and fizzy drinks. You can even cure yourself of diabetes by changing your diet and exercising.

Find a sport you love. I play tennis. Your mum and dad play squash. Try them all until you find something you enjoy. If that fails, dance.

While exercise is vital if you want to enjoy good physical health, you also need to take care of your emotional health by being still and silent sometimes. This is best achieved with meditation.

First, get in a comfortable seated position, preferably on a chair. Advanced meditators adopt the cross-legged lotus position. Not me. I do it sitting up in bed or on a chair. Then you can either focus on your breath by counting in for four, holding the breath for four (or rather not breathing in or out) and breathing out for four. You might prefer to silently repeat a mantra or special word to yourself like "ohm" or focus on a beautiful object (such as a tree, flower, beach or waterfall) and just be. Every day. For twenty minutes, if you can.

This is hard to do when you have a young family, but try it when they are asleep if that's your only window. My favorite yoga and meditation teacher in LA, Linda Carré, used to tell her class we should meditate for twenty minutes once or twice a day. "If your life is too busy to do it for twenty minutes," she said, "do it for thirty."

The results are cumulative, so the more you meditate the more calm and relaxed you will feel.

Sometimes life becomes a bit too stressful, and no amount of meditation and yoga will stop you from feeling angry or fed up. In which case, I recommend a Bach's Rescue Me Remedy lozenge or tincture. Yaca calls them "Mum's Happy Drops." I might not have survived her rebellious teenage years without them.

At some point you will probably have a yeast infection in your ladies' toilet parts. Don't worry, we all get them. I get one if I take too much vitamin C or antibiotics. Try washing the area with antidandruff shampoo as soon as it starts itching. Head & Shoulders is best. It's an anti-fungal and does the trick for me. A friend was told by their doctor to wash her leg with dandruff shampoo to get rid of a fungal skin infection. That's what gave me the idea to use it for a yeast infection (which is also a fungus).

If that doesn't work, you can buy pessaries over the counter at the pharmacy. There are one, three, five and seven day courses. Don't bother with the one day. You'll need at least three.

There will come a time (around age fifty-five) when the things that make you happiest are a good night's sleep and a decent bowel movement. After a lifetime of suffering and research, I can tell you without fear of contradiction that it's harder (no pun intended) for some people to poo than others due to their physiology, and no amount of fruit and vegetables can get them going smoothly and effectively.

A large cup of coffee in the morning, and four Super Colon Cleanse taken every evening with a glass of water have changed my life for the better. It says on the container not to use for more than two months at a time, but I have been taking them daily for years with no side effects and enormous benefit. Your dad thinks it's a terrible idea, by the way.

The worst side effect of constipation is hemorrhoids. I do not want you to be like me and suffer for thirteen years because you are too embarrassed to mention it to your doctor.

This is what I have learned. The world can be separated into three groups: those who have hemorrhoids, those who have had hemorrhoids and those who are going to have hemorrhoids.

Do not bother having an operation to have them removed as they will come back bigger, stronger and even more painful.

Preparation H with a small dab of Lanacane pain-killing cream placed you know where is as good a remedy as any. Grand Poppa C swears by tea tree oil for everything from piles to toothache, insect bites and spots.

There was a time when I would have been mortified to discuss my nether regions with anyone and suffered in silence rather than go to the doctor. It started when I was pregnant with your dad. In the olden days, the first thing you were prescribed when pregnant was iron tablets — which have the same effect as pouring concrete in your bottom.

No one told me until I was in advanced labor that you push through your bottom when you give birth. Do not do as I did with your dad and refrain from pushing for fear of pooing myself and end up with a forceps delivery.

Cut to about thirteen years after your dad was born and I had suffered regular bouts of thrombosed hemmies where it felt like someone was sticking a red-hot poker up my botticelli, but I was too embarrassed to go to the doctor until finally I could take the excruciating pain no more.

There had been a few false starts over the years when I plucked up courage and another, more handsome doctor was standing in for him, so I chickened out and pretended I was there for birth control pills.

There had also been a mortifying occasion prior to this when I had a dodgy pap smear and had to have the world's most handsome gynecologist look up my chuff.

But nothing prepared me for the horror of having to be examined by the doctor who wouldn't take my word for it that I had hemorrhoids and insisted on seeing for himself. Just when I thought my life couldn't get any worse, that very night after my anus was violated, I was the after-dinner speaker at a ladies' group meeting and was introduced by the chairperson in glowing terms as her husband, my doctor, who now knew me better than anyone else on the planet, looked on.

The good doctor had suggested I have an operation, which I finally agreed to, but only if it could be done in a hospital many miles away in a different county where no one would know me.

I shouldn't really have been surprised when the nurse who prepared me for the op recognized me as the lady who writes the women's page for the *Dorset Evening Echo*. I denied it, but she knew it was me and probably told all her mates and colleagues.

Even if she did, who cares? The important thing is that no medical issue you endure will be more embarrassing than what I've been through and from which I've lived to tell the tale. Save yourself a lot of pain and time by getting all medical problems dealt with as quickly as possible. Otherwise, you'll just be delaying the inevitable.

Life Lesson # 10   *Don't smoke. It stinks and it kills you.*

13

RELIGION

Few, if any, children over twelve believe in the existence of Father Christmas and the Tooth Fairy. I am one of the growing numbers of people who believe that eventually it will be accepted that there's no such supernatural being as God either.

The Romans and the Greeks worked out pretty quickly that Neptune and Zeus weren't for real, so it's incredible to me that the greatest, most advanced civilizations the world has ever known still believe in their god.

I think it's going to be awkward for church leaders when it finally dawns that not only is their emperor not wearing any clothes, but he doesn't exist. I do hope I live to see that day.

I can't prove He doesn't, but believers can't *prove* He exists either. And when people make extraordinary claims, it's up to them to provide the evidence. I am writing God and He, as opposed to god and he, she or it, out of respect for believers who write it like that.

It's important to respect other people's points of view even if you don't share their beliefs, especially where religion is concerned, because it's a subject people feel very strongly about.

But if people believe in fairy tales, they should expect to take some stick. It's really important, I believe, for you to at least know all sides of the argument.

Over the centuries, people with different religious beliefs have gone to war and ostracized neighbors who didn't agree with their views. They still do.

An atheist is someone who categorically believes that there is no such thing as a supernatural God who created people, life and the universe.

Agnostics are people who think that God's existence or otherwise probably cannot be known for sure, so won't commit one way or the other.

It's fair to say that the vast majority of people follow the religion of their parents and rarely take the time to understand alternative philosophies or find out what other religions actually stand for.

The important thing if you decide to follow a religion is to follow the one that makes most sense to you and not what your parents or grandparents tell you. Weigh up all the arguments and make your own decision. But, above all, be respectful of other people's views. There's no law that says you must follow a particular religion, but there are followers of all religions who will kill you for not siding with their team.

Unless they are Buddhists. Senior Buddhists say it isn't even a religion. It's more like a way of life, a philosophy with one motto: seek the truth. They also advocate kindness. It's hard to argue against that ideology, but Buddhism as it's practiced by ninety-nine percent of followers is very much a religion with temples, prayers and deities. And the Buddha recommended being kind for purely pragmatic reasons because it helps you (allegedly) along on the path to enlightenment. In practice, though, Buddhism says a lot about kindness and compassion for its own sake. It's thought to be a fruit of enlightenment as well as a means toward enlightenment.

Although even Buddhists are getting violent. Reuters news agency reported on May 29, 2013 that "security forces struggled to control Buddhist mobs who burned Muslim homes on Wednesday for a second day in the northern Myanmar city of Lashio in a dangerous widening of ultra-nationalist Buddhist violence."

This attack resulted in at least one death. More such incidents have been reported since. Historically, there have been cases of Buddhist violence, some of it primarily ethnic, but also because of disputes over doctrine.

They clearly forgot that Buddhists believe in reincarnation and karma. Karma means reaping what you sow. If you say or do something mean or unkind, eventually someone else will be mean or unkind to you. I quite like that. But Buddhists also think we keep coming back after we die (reincarnating) until we learn from our mistakes. That's where they lose me. I don't believe in reincarnation. It doesn't pass the smell test. My smell test anyway.

I believe we have one chance at life. I believe that life is not a dress rehearsal for an afterlife and we must live and love as well as we possibly can because this is it.

I do think it's important to respect and appreciate all living things. Another advantage of getting older is you take more time to smell the roses. The sooner you start noticing the extraordinary and beautiful nature all around you the better. It will make you smile on the inside.

Some of the most influential religions include Christianity, Islam, Hinduism and Judaism. There are hundreds more religions that have been created over the years. The most derogatory label you can give a religion is to call it a cult. But a cult is really just a religion without so many followers.

There are about 2.2 billion Christians in the world, 1.6 billion Muslims (followers of Islam), 1 billion Hindus and (here's the interesting figure to me) "only" around 15 million Jews.

The vast majority of God-fearing and worshiping people are good, honorable and law-abiding. They respect other religions and beliefs and want to live together in harmony. But there is an ever-growing number of what we call fundamentalists who call for the destruction of everyone who doesn't believe in the same supreme being as them.

Jews have been on the receiving end of more hatred, prejudice and bigotry than any other, although this has often been more a racial issue than a religious one. You will learn in history lessons just how cruelly the Jews have been treated over the centuries.

You will also learn in school about the horror that has been going on in the Middle East over a piece of land that used to be called Palestine where predominantly Muslim Palestinians lived that is now called Israel and has been since 1948. Historically, many Palestinians were Christians. They were a minority but a large and significant minority.

"Israel" was taken away from "Palestine" and set up as a permanent home for Jews after six million of them (yes, six million) were killed in concentration camps by Germany during the Second World War (1939 to1945).

A group of nations led by Great Britain after World War Two thought they were doing the right thing by giving the Jews their own state. But they also created hatred and resentment among Palestinians who had nowhere else to go and fought over the decades to get their land back, with the support of their fellow Muslim countries that surround teeny tiny Israel — quite a few of whom have vowed that they won't rest until Israel is given back to the Palestinians and every last Jewish man, woman and child is dead and buried.

It's not all one-sided. Many Israeli Jews aren't overly fond of Palestinians either and have treated the Palestinians they have imprisoned (ironically, in concentration camps) in an appalling manner, denying them basic human rights.

Politicians and diplomats from around the world have managed to get the two sides talking around a table a few times but even as I write Israel is bombing the shit out of Gaza and just embarked on a ground invasion because three Israeli teenagers were kidnapped and murdered by Palestinians. A Palestinian teenager was promptly burned alive in retaliation. The only possible hope for peace is that Hamas, the democratically elected party that currently governs Palestine, recognizes Israel's right to exist and that a two-state solution can be found where both sides can live in harmony.

Christians and Jews have been fighting each other for nearly two thousand years and Muslims joined their company more than one thousand years ago.

I'm reminded of a famous quote from Mahatma Gandhi, leader of the Indian National Congress in the 1940s, after India was partitioned (again by the Brits and again in 1948) to separate Hindus and Muslims. The Hindus stayed in India and Muslims were given their own state, Pakistan. Raised a Hindu and renowned for his wisdom, humility and for being a pacifist, Gandhi said, "Victory attained by violence is tantamount to a defeat, for it is momentary."

Gandhi was assassinated on January 30, 1948 by a Hindu nationalist who was resentful at what he perceived as Gandhi's sympathy for India's Muslims.

Gandhi was full of good quotes such as, "I like your Christ. I don't like Christians. They are so unlike your Christ."

Christianity is based on the life and teachings of Jesus. Most Christians believe Jesus is the actual, physical Son of God and that Jesus was born to a virgin called Mary who was impregnated by the Holy Spirit. They also believe that Jesus, God and the Holy Spirit are one and the same and, most importantly, that Jesus gave his life to save humankind and only by repenting our sins and acknowledging that Jesus is our savior can we get to Heaven. Failure to do so come Judgment Day when Jesus will (allegedly) return will result in our being sent to hell for eternity.

Christianity began as a Jewish sect in the first century AD. Jesus' followers believe that He suffered for people's sins, as he was crucified and died on a cross, then buried and resurrected from the dead to grant eternal life to those who believe in him.

I have a hunch he may not have actually died on the cross but was near death when he was taken down, remained unconscious for three days, rallied for a few last breaths and finally succumbed to his dreadful injuries.

Christians call the biographies of Jesus the Gospels. By all accounts he was a good man who did good deeds. Some say he performed miracles.

According to the New Testament, where all the stories about Jesus and his followers are found, Christians were persecuted by

Jewish religious authorities who disagreed with his teachings. Virtually all persecution of early Christians came from Roman pagans.

It wasn't until one hundred years after Jesus was born that Christians began writing down his teachings and stories about him. I suspect there were a number of exaggerations and embellishments over those years. Some religious historians aren't convinced Jesus existed at all and was invented by early Christians.

Judaism is the religion, philosophy and way of life of Jewish people. It's been around for more than five thousand years and is the oldest surviving monotheistic religion. A monotheistic religion is one that only believes in and worships one deity.

Jews believe God revealed his laws and commandments to Moses on Mount Sinai and they are written down in the Hebrew bible, called the Tanakh. The first five books, Genesis through Deuteronomy, are called the Torah. Jews believe they should pray to their God and only Him. They do not follow the teachings of Jesus and do not consider him to be their savior. They don't consider Moses to be their savior either, but do consider him their greatest prophet.

As with Christianity and Islam, some Jews follow their religious laws and commandments more strictly than others. Most Jews live in Israel, America and Canada with a few million living in Europe, South America and Asia.

People who are believers in the religion of Islam are called Muslims. Their core beliefs are that there is only one God, Allah, (monotheistic again) and that Muhammad is their prophet who conveyed all Allah's teachings as told to him by the archangel Gabriel on numerous occasions between 610 CE and his death on June 8, 632 CE (CE is the same as BC, and sometimes CE is used so as not to offend non-Christians. CE is an abbreviation of Common Era, but denotes the same era as BC – Before Christ. Sometimes it's written as B.C.E. – Before the Common Era).

Mohammed was reputedly illiterate. His followers wrote down what he told them. Those teachings are written in the Muslim scripture called the Qur'an or Koran. Muslims believe Muhammad to be the last in a series of great prophets starting with Adam and including Abraham, Moses and Jesus. They also believe in the Resurrection and a Judgment Day.

Like all religions, Muslims have split up into different sects. The vast majority of Muslims are Sunni. The largest minority group of Muslims is the Shia. Sunni and Shia have fought each other frequently over the years, but since Israel was established in 1948, have found enemies in common – Jews and Westerners. Muslims consider Westerners corrupt largely because they believe they aren't sufficiently religious, not because they are Christian.

Most Muslims live in the Middle East, Central Asia, Indonesia and sub-Saharan Africa. The vast majority of Muslims are peaceful and law-abiding, but a rather scary and increasing number have called for the destruction of Israel and the United States of America.

There are Persian miniatures of Muhammad, some with his face veiled, but, at this time in history, there is a zealous refusal to represent Muhammad and it is considered a sin to draw or paint Him, a sin punishable by death.

Hinduism is an old religion with most practitioners living on the Indian sub-continent or of Indian descent. They don't have scripture as such, but many traditions have been handed down over four thousand years to form the basis. No single person is credited with developing this faith that has many sects, rituals and practices.

The Vedas, Aranyakas and Upanishads are accounts and advice written by spiritually advanced mystics over the centuries, several *thousand* years actually, from which Hinduism comes.

Simply put, and accepting there is a lot more to it than this, Hindus worship many different gods (polytheistic) that all lead to the ultimate, Brahman, which they consider to be the ultimate reality. Hinduism is about the search for liberation that can be achieved through meditation, yoga and prayer.

They believe that life has four stages: student, householder, retiree and renunciant. Fame and fortune is applauded — as is the pursuit of pleasure — but, near the end of your life, you let it all go, which will put you on the path of spiritual liberation.

Hindus believe in the sanctity of all life, and many are

vegetarians. They also believe in reincarnation and karma; and understand and appreciate that other religions are relevant and should be respected.

Buddhism is a spin-off of Hinduism. Around 500 BCE, Siddhartha Gautama renounced his wealthy lifestyle in India (and abandoned his wife and baby) in search of spiritual liberation, known as Nirvana (from the ancient language of Sanskrit).

The meaning of life eluded him for many years until he sat under a bodhi tree determined not to move until he became enlightened. On the forty-ninth day, he opened his eyes, having realized through meditation that the problem with humanity is that we are all deluded and ego-driven; and that the sooner we ditch the three bad habits of desire, anger and ignorance, the better.

Siddhartha, known as the Buddha (the Awakened One), spent the next forty-five years teaching his wisdom to monks and nuns, promoting a solitary and spiritual way of life. He insisted his disciples must not write anything down, so his most important sermons were conveyed orally. It wasn't until hundreds of years after his death that the Buddha's teachings were finally committed to paper.

The earliest surviving accounts of the Buddha's teachings are in Pali, an ancient northwestern Indian dialect. I suspect a lot was lost in the translation.

That said, the message of Buddhism is one of love, peace and non-violence, so I've no idea what the Buddhists in Indonesia are thinking. If they didn't believe in reincarnation and weren't so fond of chanting, I'd probably lean towards Buddhism. But an excellent book, *Dakini Power* by Michaela Haas (who tells the stories of twelve leading Buddhist women) and a couple of other things concern me.

While most of the stories are extraordinary, humbling and inspiring, it bothers me that the boss man of the Buddhist center funded by the writing talents and shared wisdom of the most famous female Buddhist, Pema Chödrön, makes her spend hours outside the compound dusting rocks to keep her humble.

It bothers me more that Pema agrees to do it. I'd hand the shovel to the boss man. I'd like to think she wouldn't do it if she didn't want to.

All religious hierarchies are prejudiced against women. Prejudice comes from ignorance and should be resisted at every turn.

It's not possible to give even a thumbnail sketch of every religion, because there are so many of them, but I am going to talk about two more. Firstly, Mormonism because your mum belongs to that church so it's likely you will be introduced to it at some point. Your other grandmother, your mum's mum, a wonderful woman who you call Nau, is a Baptist and a regular church-goer.

The Mormon Church is also called the Church of Latter Day Saints. Incidentally, Grand Poppa C's father, (your step-great grandfather) is a Mormon.

This religion is based on Christianity. They use the same bible, the King James version, while the Book of Mormon and a couple of other historical documents are also considered sacred scriptures.

Mormonism was started by a man called Joseph Smith in the early 1820s. Mormons consider him a prophet. Smith claimed, and millions of people subsequently believed, that while Christianity has basis in truth, it got sidetracked and departed from ancient wisdom.

When Joseph Smith was seventeen, he claims God sent him an angel called Moroni who told him that a collection of ancient writings, engraved on golden plates by ancient prophets, was buried in a nearby hill in Wayne County, New York.

The writings described a people whom God had led from Jerusalem to the western hemisphere six hundred years before Jesus' birth. Allegedly, Moroni was the last prophet among those people and had buried the record, which God had promised to bring forth in the latter days. Hence, "latter day saints."

Smith said he was instructed by Moroni to meet at the hill every September 22 to receive further instructions. Four years after the first visit, in 1827, he was allowed to take the plates and was directed to translate them into English from ancient Egyptian.

It's not known how he did that, never having studied ancient Egyptian. There were eleven witnesses who swore they saw the original plates. Smith's neighbor and one of the witnesses, Martin

Harris, mortgaged his farm to pay for the printing of the Book of Mormon.

Mr. and Mrs. Harris repeatedly asked Smith to lend them the plates that had been translated so they could touch them as and when they fancied. Smith caved under the pressure and Mrs. Harris subsequently lost those first one hundred and sixteen plates. Some say she stole them.

Mr. Smith was so upset about Mrs. Harris's carelessness (or theft) that he was no longer able to translate the rest of the plates. So Angel Moroni took them back until Smith repented. Which he did and the translation was resumed. Miraculously, Smith, with help from a man called Oliver Cowdery, managed to finish the job in two months and returned the plates to Moroni who buried them somewhere safe. So safe, they've never been found since.

Skeptics believe Joseph Smith made some of it up and stole the rest from other books, mostly the King James Bible. I'm firmly with the skeptics on this.

Some of the Mormons' older practices, like having as many wives as they want, have been largely banned. As far as I can tell, the Mormons' biggest difference from mainstream Christianity is they don't believe God and Jesus are one and the same.

They also believe that their church is the only true and living church because of the divine authority God gave Smith and that Smith and his successors are modern prophets who receive revelation from God on how to guide their church.

Mormons believe that life on earth is just a brief part of an eternal existence and that people originally existed as spirits or "intelligences" before God offered us the chance to live on earth as humans.

While Mormons believe in the general accuracy of the King James Bible, they also believe it's incomplete and contains errors that are corrected in the Book of Mormon, which they hold to be divine scripture and equal in authority to the Bible.

The first LDS missionaries arrived in Fiji in 1893 and quickly spread their beliefs. Rather alarmingly, the Mormon Church in America didn't allow in black people until 1978.

I've been to several services at the church in Vivili, near your mum and dad's house. I go for the incredible singing and to meet the wonderful villagers.

I was brought up as a Jehovah's Witness until I was nine years old, so I can speak from experience.

Their bible is also the King James version and their religion is based on Christianity. I had weekly bible studies (on a Wednesday evening) with Brother Arthur Napier and went to regular services at our local Kingdom Hall.

Yes, I have known the emotional pain and shame of having a door slammed in my face. Even at the tender age of five, I rather sympathized with people who were having their privacy interrupted by complete strangers wanting to convert them, however friendly and smiling we were.

Reading the book of Revelation was, well, the final revelation for me. Here is such a vengeful and wrathful God that I didn't like him at all and didn't think he was worthy of my worship.

Here's the worst part: JWs don't celebrate birthdays or Christmas, considering them Pagan activities. I confess, having doors slammed in my face and not getting presents for Christmas or my birthday until I was nine have had a long and lasting detrimental effect on me.

The door slamming makes it difficult for me to ask for things. I sometimes assist at charitable events but can't be the person who asks companies or people for donations. I could never work in telesales.

My mum was the one who was really into the religion. I think my dad went along with it to keep her happy. It was he who relented and bought me a camera for my ninth birthday, bringing me much joy and incurring the wrath of Brother Arthur Napier who said our family was no longer welcome at the Kingdom Hall and I wasn't worthy of his bible study time. Glory be.

I remember thinking before I was nine that it is ridiculous that JWs take the bible verse "thou shalt not take another man's blood" to mean refusing a life-saving blood transfusion when it clearly just means don't kill anyone in the language of old. When that was written, you couldn't even get a blood transfusion, as they hadn't been invented.

And let's not forget the day the JWs predicted would be Armageddon and Judgment Day has been and gone without event.

I have never been able to get my parents to explain why they bought into the JW doctrine or how they felt about getting kicked out for buying me a camera. We started celebrating Christmas that year as well. Presents for all. Fantastic.

My younger siblings never knew the disappointment, shame and embarrassment of explaining to their school friends why they didn't get a present for their birthday or Christmas. Actually, neither did I. I used to pretend to school friends I got all sorts of amazing stuff my parents couldn't afford.

Christmas is now my favorite time of year. I'm only in it for the presents, though. Mum still opens the door to JWs, and buys their magazines, *Awake* and *Watchtower*.

My dad is eighty-five as I write this. He hopes there is a heaven and that when the time comes he will be admitted.

I've heard religious people say we need religion to give people a sense of morality. I don't buy that. I don't think we have to worship anyone or anything to live a good and moral life.

You might think someone must have created this amazing world.

I don't. I believe in evolution. I think it is just part of the miracle and wonder of life and human beings are capable of being moral and ethical without adhering to a religion or worshipping a god. That doesn't make me a bad person, it makes me a secular humanist.

Just know that I will love you no matter what you choose to believe.

After careful thought, research and consideration, I believe that Jesus might have existed, Mohammed and Buddha for sure. I believe they were spiritually advanced, righteous human beings. But over the centuries, their teachings have been misinterpreted, exaggerated and exploited by others.

Which part of the world you were born in - and what your parents believed and therefore taught you - usually determines which religion, if any, you will follow. And while I don't agree with atheist Christopher Hitchens that religion poisons everything, I do agree it poisons a lot.

I believe this to be true about all religions, that their original leaders and prophets all believed the same things were important: love and kindness.

Life Lesson # 11 *Question everything and make up your own mind, especially where religion is concerned.*

Recommended further reading: *The Complete Idiot's Guide To The World's Religions* by Brandon Torporov and Father Luke Buckle; *The World's Religions* by Huston Smith, *The Story of Thought* by Bryan Magee; *god Is Not Great: How Religion Poisons Everything* by Christopher Hitchens, *The God Delusion* by Richard Dawkins and *The Prophet* by Kahlil Gibran.

You with your proud parents on your 1st birthday

You with your mother and grandmothers

Great Aunt Julia and Marley have fun in Fiji

You with your other grandmother, Nau, on your first birthday wearing your Fijian ceremonial clothes. First and sixteenth birthdays are big deals in Fiji. I wonder how we will celebrate your sweet sixteenth? Fun and fabulously is my guess.

You, me and Grand Poppa C

You with your namesake in LA

You with your parents and other grandparents: Tukai, Grandpa, Grandma and Nau

14

LIVING CONSCIOUSLY

I know people, good people, who truly believe that their God talks to them and answers their prayers. They say they clearly hear His voice telling them what to do and what not to do.

I believe, with little or no scientifically proven facts or independent studies to back me up, that the God people hear talking to them is their conscience and we all have one to varying degrees, depending on how open we are. We all possess the ability to rationalize situations in our mind and we should all listen to what our own inner voice of wisdom and reason tells us.

This is not to say that if a voice in our head tells us to kill someone or blow up a building that we must do it. There are clear boundaries of right and wrong.

Let's assume I'm not completely nuts and may be on to something, so please bear with me and hear/read me out.

First, here's my understanding of what it is to live a conscious life: to be balanced in mind and body to such a degree that things fall into place for us and seemingly impossible dreams and wishes sometimes come true. And when things don't go as we'd hoped or planned, we're fine with it because we trust in the process of life.

I still have some way to go, because situations and people do still piss me off on occasion, but that's happening less and less as I get older.

I'm a work in progress and don't have the meaning of life all figured out yet. But I'm hoping you will heed some of my advice, learn from my experiences and errors of judgment and live your best possible life.

If you become financially secure and don't have to work, follow your passion and help make the world a better place. Set yourself goals. Be focused on your goals. Learn new skills. Have a hobby. Be kind.

I'm a list maker. Once I've ticked off everything on my list of jobs and things I want to achieve, I make a new list. I also believe that sometimes we manifest our own reality with our thoughts and words.

Are you wondering, "Well, if you're so bloody good at manifesting, how come you and Grand Poppa C live in a one-bedroom apartment and not a ranch like Southfork?"

That's a fair and reasonable question and I confess I don't know why, either. There's still time. I can tell you this: when Grand

Poppa C came to live with me in Los Angeles, we were technically homeless. Not "living in a cardboard box" homeless, but we didn't have our own place. We were able to use a friend's fabulous apartment as a base because this friend travelled a lot and was often away.

We'd move out leaving the place spotless and with no sign we had been there then move back in when he left on his travels again. During that first year, we stayed in twenty-five different places (all fabulous). Our friend only gave us a day or two's warning he was coming back, but within a few hours of us hearing he was on his way, someone would call us to see if we could house-, dog- or cat-sit while they went away for a couple of weeks.

There was only once or maybe twice when we didn't have anywhere to go and were able to stay with GAJ, Arthur and the newly born Marley, who we loved and adored and were able to properly bond with.

It wasn't exactly fun packing up and unloading all our worldly goods into the back of our PT Cruiser time and time again, but we were able to see the positive side that we were going to stay in amazing homes rent-free rather than bemoan our not having our own home yet. When we were able to afford our own place after that first year, it made us appreciate it all the more.

I have no doubt that success and happiness can be measured by how we react to our failures and disappointments. Even in the face of great adversity and rejection, the law of averages alone says things will probably get better.

But don't be too chipper all the time, especially when things are totally crappy and you have taken one too many metaphorical punches to the gut in a relatively short space of time because that's not being authentic and people will see right through you. It can also be rather annoying to others when people wear a beatific, fake smile.

That's easy for me to say because I have GAJ and Yaca and they have me. We can tell each other anything and even behave unreasonably (me much more than them) but the other will listen without judgment, give advice and still love the other unconditionally. To know you are loved unconditionally is extremely comforting.

I recommend starting each day from a place of gratitude for what you have rather than moan about what you don't have. If I can't think of anything positive to be grateful for that happened to me the day before, then I give thanks that I have two arms and two legs or that I don't have toothache. I aim for five things to be thankful for.

Having a positive and happy outlook does attract more good people and opportunities into your life. Even if you're not a fundamentally happy person (and I know you are, because you are always laughing and jumping for joy), you can train yourself to be more positive. If you live and work with permanently miserable Moaning Minnies that will rub off on you after a while. Bad habits can be broken. Just replace them with good ones, and replace Moaning Minnies and Debbie Downers with Happy Harriets.

Of course, life's not always easy and wishes don't always come true. When we were looking to buy our first car, Grand Poppa C said he didn't mind what car we leased so long as it wasn't black or a PT Cruiser. Did I mention the PT Cruiser we leased was black? It was the only car immediately available in Santa Monica at a price we could afford. Its hatchback body was perfect for loading and unloading our stuff.

But another time, Grand Poppa C's wishes did come true. His dream car is a Porsche 911 for fun and a Mercedes-Benz or Audi as a family car. Grand Poppa C knows a thing or two about cars because he writes about them. The first Christmas he came to visit me in Los Angeles, he was loaned a Porsche 911 and a Mercedes-Benz by the manufacturers to ferry your dad and Yaca around in while they were here visiting.

I used to write affirmations regularly in a big black book, but stopped doing that when I didn't land the job I really wanted, had avidly affirmed for and was absolutely convinced I was going to get.

It was to be the co-presenter with Chris Evans on a morning television program starting on Channel 4 called *The Big Breakfast Show.*

A talent agent got me an audition for it. I was one of four women who were called back for a second audition, which I failed because I spoke out loud to the director in the gallery when I was thrown a question in my earpiece to ask the family I was interviewing.

At that time, I'd never done any live TV and didn't know presenters are always getting spoken to from the production gallery and must never react, just silently do what the director or producer says. Not say out loud, "OK, will do."

Later Chris Evans told me I would never know just how close I was to getting the job, which rather implied that it was down to me and Gaby Roslin, who did get it. Later, when I started working in television news doing live reports I was easily able to deal with the constant instructions from directors coming through my earpiece.

I was looking at my old big black affirmations book the other day. Flicking through it, I stumbled upon a page filled with this handwritten affirmation, "I give thanks that I get *The Big Breakfast Show* under grace and in a perfect way." It was dated July 31, 1992.

It was either Florence Scovel Shinn or another great metaphysician, manifester and positive thinker Louise L. Hay (probably both) who advise always affirming for things in the present tense as if you already have them and ask for them under grace and in a perfect way. Otherwise, for example, Gaby Roslin might have met a nasty accident thereby making the presenter situation vacant. Or if you affirm for money and don't ask for it in a perfect way, then it might come as an inheritance from the death of a beloved relative.

Back to *The Big Breakfast*. I chuckled when I read my wish to work on that show, because I did. Seven years on, when I worked at ITN, they produced the news for *The Big Breakfast*. I was the news producer and reporter there for two years, and the program news editor every Sunday when the two main journalists had the night off. It might be a tad tenuous and it wasn't the job I affirmed for (I wasn't exactly clear which job I wanted and you do have to spell it out), but I did get to work on *The Big Breakfast*.

That was my last job before I moved to Los Angeles. Shortly after that, ITN lost the *Big Breakfast* contract (not because I left, I hasten to add) and another show I worked on, *The Early Morning News*, was canceled, so I'd have been out of a job anyway.

This is an excellent example of things working out for the best. I moved to LA to live with GAJ for a year and to begin the next chapter of my life.

Living with GAJ was fantastic until she went on vacation to Fiji and brought back a dog, Muttley, who proceeded to ruin my life by eating my favorite things. But I wrote a book based on the experience and I grew to love Muttley so good things can come from bad experiences and first impressions about animals and people can be wrong.

I did the occasional report for ITN from LA, which is how I got my first five-year visa. My main creative outlet was writing the book, *Plus One: A Year In The Life Of A Hollywood Nobody,* then promoting it and writing articles.

There was plenty of travel and adventure with GAJ. As I've mentioned, we each had a gentleman caller and life was sweet for four years.

The book was about my adventures in LA with GAJ and going everywhere as her plus one – the nameless nobody invited to openings and parties as somebody's guest.

A filmmaker, Mary McGuckian, optioned *Plus One* to make a movie based on it, but that fell through until she decided to make a mockumentary about trying to get my book made into a movie.

I did get paid ($10,000) for use of title and GAJ and I played ourselves for about five minutes in two scenes. *The Making of Plus One* wasn't a box office success but GAJ and I did shoot our scenes in the south of France, the film was launched at the Cannes film festival and we had an absolute blast. Top actors like Jennifer Tilly, Amanda Plummer, Geraldine Chaplin and John Sessions were in it, and we got to hang and work with them. One of our best-ever adventures.

Now what was completely shocking and disappointing was that *Plus One* the book wasn't as big a publishing success as *Bridget Jones' Diary*, which is what I had been affirming for. And having read Deepak Chopra's *The Spontaneous Fulfillment of Desire*, and followed Dr. Chopra's recommendations to the letter by building an altar where I placed effigies of archetypes (Krishna, Lakshmi, Durgha, Ganesha and St. Clare the patron saint of television) along with nine semi-precious stones placed in a vase of soil from a rich man's garden, a three-legged frog and three Chinese coins on a piece of red silk thread, I felt cheated by the cosmos.

I know what you're thinking. Isn't this suspiciously like praying to a god, specifically four Hindu deities and a saint. And, one might be forgiven for wondering, a tad hypocritical for someone who claims nothing but disdain for all forms of worship?

If it's all the same to you, I prefer to think of it more as a statement of intent that all my dreams and wishes should come true and all my needs be met.

Then I got sucked into *The Secret* by Rhonda Byrne, the next in a long line of self-help books whose main achievement is to make a ton of money for the author. But they all have a thread of truth to them.

Ms. Byrne suggests that all we need to do is ask God (I prefer to ask the Cosmos or the Universe) for what we want, believe it will happen, and wait to receive. Because categorically and absolutely we can manifest everything we want and all our dreams will come true, she says, without seemingly lifting a finger.

Ms. Byrne doesn't mention that we also need to set our intention and work toward our goals. Or that life sometimes throws us a curve ball that spoils our plans and forces us to change direction. It isn't enough to simply wish or pray for things and events. If prayer worked, everybody would be doing it. Set yourself goals.

That said, there's some wisdom in Ms. Byrne's book and she also advises starting each day from a place of gratitude. As do all self-help authors of any note.

Another positive thinker is my friend and former neighbor, CJ. We were walking along the beach together one day and she was gently chastising me for worrying about needing a car while assuring me one would turn up if I only asked the Universe. She suggested I give thanks for one right then and there, which I did.

Before we had reached Santa Monica pier, CJ slapped her forehead with the palm of her hand. "You can use Mike's Porsche for six months while he's away in Europe."

A brand-new Porsche 911. Have I mentioned how lucky I am?

Yet still my Reality TV show ideas weren't getting picked up. I partnered with four different producers over five years to pitch my ideas to production companies.

Our pitches were met with interest, but no one bought the ideas, and time and time again we were told it was all about who was attached to the project.

You can imagine my frustration when none of my creative projects were coming to fruition and I was still struggling financially. So I boxed up my archetypes and lucky charms, shoved them at the back of my bedside cabinet and said, "How do you like them apples, Universe?" and proceeded to carry on with my life by being content with what I did have and taking joy in the way things are. "Living in the now" is another way of putting it.

I still began each day with meditation, some yoga stretches and by giving thanks for my life of health, wealth, love, happiness and creativity.

Over the course of my journalistic career, I have sometimes had to interview astrologers, tarot card readers and psychics, or consulted with one if they were at a friend's party. With one exception (an Irish psychic called Patrick and that was probably coincidence), not one of their predictions has ever come true.

The unhappiest women I know are the ones who spend the most money on consulting such people. Don't waste your time or money on them.

If there was any truth to astrology, then twins, triplets, etc - all babies who were part of multiple births - would go on to lead identical lives. They don't.

That said, I do believe that humans have a telepathic ability (some much more than others) that hasn't been fully explored.

GAJ and I went to a talk by Marianne Williamson in LA. She's one of the world's most successful authors, spiritual teachers and lecturers. We said hello afterwards. We'd met before, when Marianne had come to one of Julia's gigs in New York. Marianne said we should get together again soon.

GAJ, Marianne and I spent a wonderful two hours together drinking tea and eating chocolate cake at Sweet Lady Jane's on Montana.

I like Marianne and greatly admire her intellect, ideas on prison reform and how she wants to change the political landscape by changing the conversation from what's best for the economy to what's best for humanity.

We met a couple more times during her (unsuccessful) bid to win the District 33 seat for Congress, and I bought her latest book, *The Law of Divine Compensation: On Work, Money and Miracles*. It was while reading this book that it dawned on me that I hadn't been grateful enough, if at all, that my greatest wish in life has always been that your dad and Yaca would be happy and healthy. And they are.

It's not for me to tell you about their trials and tribulations, but there have been times when I've been worried sick about them both, especially Yaca. So my greatest, indeed my only wish for some years, had come true. But I had never taken the time to properly express my genuine gratitude for that when I did my daily gratitude ritual.

It's not about saying thanks to a "god" but having a genuine feeling and sense of gratitude for what you have.

I stopped wishing for things. I had everything.

I always felt Joan Rivers would be the best host for one of my shows in particular. One producing partner said she could get to Joan. She knew someone who knew someone who knew her agent, but nothing came of it. We never got past the agent's assistant's assistant at the William Morris Endeavor Agency.

That show, along with a slew of my other brilliantly creative ideas, went on the back burner and I forgot all about it.

I was flying back to LA with GAJ and Marley after a trip to England, but we couldn't get three seats together, so I had to sit four rows back. We were quite miffed with the lady who sat beside GAJ in an aisle seat who wouldn't change with me even though I had an aisle seat as well and it was absolutely no skin off her nose to swap.

I soon realized that one advantage of being separated from my family was the fact the seat next to me was empty and I would be able to lie across it. Except just as the captain instructed the crew to secure the doors, a tall, dark and handsome young man fell through door with seconds to spare.

Of course he sat next to me and of course he was Joan Rivers' senior producer on E!'s *Fashion Police*.

We have formed a partnership to produce one of my TV show ideas. I said to him at our first meeting what an extraordinary coincidence it was that we sat next to each other. He shook his head and said, "I don't believe in coincidences."

In between developing my Reality TV show idea and shooting a sizzle reel, I began writing this book for you. As the words poured out, I began thinking there might be a wider audience for it.

I was waiting for a friend in Cecconi's restaurant and musing that if the book did get published, I would need some author recommendations and how Marianne Williamson would be ideal. It had been six months since our tea and I didn't feel comfortable reaching out and asking for a big favor when I didn't know her well enough.

As I left the restaurant, I bumped into Marianne. She'd been having lunch at the same place, with the actress Jane Lynch and I had no idea she was there.

Jane remembered having met me before with GAJ when they both performed at a charity event and Marianne suggested we all get together again for tea. Oh, alright then.

Coincidence? You be the judge.

But I absolutely and categorically do not believe there is a supreme being up in the sky watching over us and making decisions about who lives, who dies, who is lucky and healthy and who isn't. Sometimes, though, you can be in the flow and life goes well. Good times. Enjoy and make the most of them.

Life Lesson # 12 *Things don't always work out for the best, but they do work out.*

15

GHOST IN THE MACHINE

If I had a dollar for every person I've met who tells me their life story should be a book, I'd have $278 by now. The great thing about self-publishing is that everyone can write their life story and turn it into a book. The terrible thing about self-publishing is that everyone can write their life story and turn it into a book.

The difficulty is explaining to civilians (non-celebrities) that the chances of their getting an advance from a major publisher to write their book are slim to none. Some people, however, just want to tell their life story for family and friends, so they will know how he or she lived, and how their experiences made them the person they became, like this one I'm writing for you.

The thing is, most people can't write for toffee. They might be able to conjugate a verb, but can they tell their tale or share their brilliant idea so people will flock into bookstores (the few that are left) for a hard copy (so last millennium) or buy a downloadable version of their book? Can they make a story so compelling that you can't stop reading? That's where ghostwriters come in.

I've been earning a reasonable living helping other people write their books. I ask the subject of the book pertinent and relevant questions in a relaxed, conversational manner that will jog his or her memory, which should then help furnish those extra details that give depth and authenticity. Then I shape the text so it flows, retaining the person's voice and conveying exactly what they want to say in a way that can keep a reader's attention.

People don't realize how much work goes into editing out the boring and mundane stuff, and making sense of what's been said. In conversation, you can also read body language, facial expressions and hear intonation to get someone's drift. But what sounds scintillating and riveting can sometimes be almost nonsense when seen written down.

While I believe a good writer can turn any story into a cracking good read with universal appeal, it's rare to meet that person who has lived a truly extraordinary life. When it last happened to me, I was on the receiving end of my first non-invasive facelift by Martha Weinstein at her salon in Brentwood, California.

I sat up during the (painless and relaxing) procedure when Martha said she was eighty-nine years old. I peered at her wrinkle-free face. She certainly didn't look it.

Then she told me she had been in the health and beauty business for almost seventy years, was known as the Argentine Oprah in her home country following the success of her TV show that ran there for twenty years, and had met Adolf Hitler, Benito Mussolini and Juan Peron as a child. I told her she really should write a book.

"I started one a few years ago," said Martha. "And I've been looking for someone to help me finish it."

I sat up for the second time, turned to her and said, "Martha, this is your lucky day."

But it was actually my lucky day as we began collaborating on *The Stay Young Revolution: How To Transform Fear of Aging Into Confidence of Youth*. Martha wanted her book to be solely about holding back the years without resorting to invasive fillers or cosmetic surgery, but there are thousands of health and beauty tomes out there fighting for attention. I convinced her it should also be part-memoir, as she has lived an amazing life that will inspire and motivate people. I doubt there's another one written by someone aged eighty-nine who speaks six languages, still works part-time as a beautician and has encountered a trifecta of fascist dictators.

The working experience with Martha was hugely enjoyable. She has excellent recall and had already written some passages that just needed editing and incorporating. I have become a proud member of Martha's Stay Young Revolution and a friendship has been forged.

I'm looking forward to Martha's ninetieth birthday party, when she will dance the tango. There's no point in urging her to start taking things easy. Martha believes keeping busy and having a purpose helps keep her youthful and beautiful. I think she has a point, so I intend to follow her example.

Meanwhile, Joan River's producer, Steve, introduced me to his business partner, Joe, and we agreed to work together to make a sizzle reel (taster) for one of my Reality TV show ideas, *The Real Bitches of Beverly Hills.*

This is the pitch: the most pampered creatures in Beverly Hills aren't the rich and famous, their dogs are. Don't think for one minute you know how far people will go to pamper their pets and buy their puppies' love. Nannies, diamond collars, mink beds, chiropractors, psychiatrists, dieticians, psychics and massage therapists, Beverly Hills dogs have it all.

Because of Steve and Joe's work commitments, they were only available to film on Fridays. So it took three months to choose and then film the cast and edit the sizzle reel. But it was worth the wait. The six-minute sizzle is truly superb.

Then we had to get representation. You can't just call up a network and make an appointment to pitch your show idea. It took a while but a top management company is shopping it for us.

The first pitch meetings at E!, A&E, OWN and Bravo went well but the people we pitched to didn't give anything away and said they'd be in touch after they discussed it with their colleagues. The bad news is we haven't heard back from them yet. Show business is slow business.

Dogs are a 118 billion-dollar industry that TV isn't really tapping right now. If the show is picked up by Bravo, we can call it *The Real Bitches of Beverly Hills* as they own the Real Housewives franchises. Everything is crossed.

We have two other pitch meetings left in the diary, with ABC and CBS. These meetings take so long to set up and then sometimes get postponed at the last minute and have to be rescheduled. Patience is a virtue I am trying to acquire. To be on a major network would mean more viewers which bring bigger budgets. Realistically, our show doesn't have a high enough production value for a major network but stranger things have happened.

I'm on quite a roll right now. I just finished co-authoring Martha's book and have been recommended to another lady who has a story she wants help writing. We've had one meeting and she said she wants to proceed.

This is another extraordinary octogenarian who used to be a singer with the big swing bands of the 1940s, including Benny Goodman, Hal McIntyre and Skitch Henderson. She was friends with Frank Sinatra and had a brilliant career touring the world with these bands, but gave it all up for love when she married her husband at age twenty-five to raise four children.

I asked her if she had any regrets about giving up her successful career. She said she doesn't. Not one bit.

I remember writing an article about the Women's Royal Voluntary Service for *The Dorset Evening Echo* and how they needed volunteers to help with their meals on wheels program.

I realized I could spare two hours a week to collect some giant containers of food and deliver them to a lunch club for other volunteers to serve to local senior citizens.

One of those volunteers was eighty-six and almost blind, yet she was cheerful and happily serving meals to able-bodied but depressed-looking women in their early sixties. I vowed to myself that I would be the one doing the serving and not the receiving when I was in my eighties. It felt to me that it wasn't a financial issue but an attitude that separated these women.

In one of Anthony Robbins' self-help books, he describes a scenario where two women were recently widowed at sixty-five. They were both in good health and had enjoyed happy marriages, but when their husbands died they had different attitudes. They were each devastated at their loss, but one chose to get her affairs in order, as she assumed her life would end soon. And guess what? It did.

The other was grateful for her happy marriage but decided to take the opportunity to try some new experiences and travel. She was climbing mountains well into her nineties.

Please never forget that living a successful and happy life isn't about being rich or famous. I always carry in my purse this definition of success: *What is success? To laugh often and much; to win the respect of intelligent people and the affection of children; to earn the appreciation of honest critics and endure the betrayal of false friends; to appreciate beauty; to find the best in others; to leave the world a bit better, whether by a healthy child, a garden patch or a redeemed social condition; to know even one life has breathed easier because you have lived; this is to have succeeded.*

Life Lesson # 13 *Age is just a number. You're never too old to live your dreams.*

Recommended further reading: *Awaken the Giant Within* by Anthony Robbins.

16

MONEY

My friend Shelley O'Connor has a theory that no one has every aspect of their lives sorted, that everyone has at least one area where they struggle. At first I thought she was talking rubbish, but the more I thought about it, the more I realized she might be right.

I know wealthy and successful people who are incapacitated by depression or a physical ailment. Others who seem to have it all but have never found love or hate their job. With me, it's money. I have limped from month to month financially most of my life. I am abundant in all other areas, but financial security has always eluded me.

I usually juggle a mountain of credit card debt. On the positive side, I am good at it and can give you this one important piece of financial advice: always pay more than the minimum required each month, even if it's just a few dollars. Because that compounded credit card interest is almost impossible to pay off if you just pay the minimum.

If you do amass debt, pay it off as soon as possible. Preferably, don't even go into debt in the first place and save up for something you want rather than go into debt to buy it.

Financial guru Suze Orman has an excellent piece of advice for people struggling with debt or low income: before you buy something, ask yourself *is it a want or a need?* If it's a want and not a need, then don't buy it.

I do see light at the end of the tunnel, though. Once my Reality TV show gets picked up, I'll be able to pay off the credit cards and never be in debt again, because networks will be fighting over my many other TV show ideas. That's the hope anyway.

Financially and creatively, things have taken a turn for the better already with my latest book collaboration.

We've had three interview sessions so far and I am thoroughly enjoying working with this lady. Not just because she pays me on time. Her story is extraordinary. She was at Julliard with Miles Davis and has some great anecdotes about Frank Sinatra and Sammy Davis Jr., and touring Europe with Benny Goodman in the 1940s.

The best way to achieve financial security is by your own efforts, not by marrying or inheriting it. I know people who have inherited wealth and feel so guilty about it that they can't enjoy it.

I have noticed that some women (and men for that matter) who have wealthy and successful spouses rarely see them because they are always working and/or feel that because they pay the bills they have a license to sleep around; so there can be a lot of heartbreak that comes with marrying money.

Best not to be beholden to anyone else and make your own money so you can be financially independent. But if you do fall in love with and marry a wonderful person who just happens to be loaded, I will breathe a sigh of relief because I do not want you to have to struggle to get by.

Then again, I do want you to struggle for a little bit so you will fully appreciate money when you earn it. I hope you will be generous with any good fortune you may achieve and help others less fortunate than yourself. But not so extravagant that you fritter it away. I've known rich people who are frugal bordering on miserly. It's a fine balance.

Accepting that good health and happiness are paramount, financial security comes a close third. Who am I kidding? I think I'd put it at the top, because when you have money you have choices.

If you are sick, you can afford to buy the best treatments and medical advice and plenty of dosh enables you to pay for holidays and other fun activities that will put a smile on your face.

Of course, there are plenty of fun activities that are free, but you get my drift.

There's a wonderful video *What If Money Was No Object?* by Alan

Watts, a British Philosopher. I like it. Check it out on YouTube. I wouldn't change a thing about my life apart from having a bit more moolah to my name. I'd be living my life exactly like it is: same husband, same career, same family and friends with just a few more massages, facials and dinners out.

I'm not even sure I'd fly first class every time I crossed the Atlantic even if I could afford it. Virgin had a special on at Christmas when I went back to England to see Yaca and for my parents' sixtieth wedding anniversary. I could upgrade to first class (from economy) at check-in for £500. This felt like a once-in-a-lifetime opportunity and the very reason why credit cards were invented in the first place.

I flew first class before with GAJ when she had gigs in The Philippines and Japan and I recall it being a wonderful experience that I longed to repeat. It suited me very well.

This was my chance to do it again. And, if you believe such things, by upgrading I was telling the Cosmos that I had every faith that my Reality TV show would get picked up and money (or lack thereof) would no longer be an issue for me.

It was January 1 and I had vowed to not drink alcohol for the entire month, which was a pity because the fine wine and cocktails would have flowed during the entire flight if I had wanted them to; but a vow is a vow.

The food was superb, but the flat bed was hard, the mattress too thin and the young people (in their thirties) who had also upgraded at check-in were determined to have their money's worth and drink Sir Richard Branson dry. They were happy, but they were loud and borderline obnoxious throughout the flight, so sleep was impossible.

The experience wasn't worth going into debt for. Don't be a financial fool like me. Ask yourself, *Is it a want or a need?*

I am enormously proud of your dad and Yaca not least because they are both debt free.

Not sure how Grand Poppa C and I can get our expenses down any further. We've downsized from a one-bedroom to a smaller one-bedroom apartment and are now a one-car family. I did a three-month survey a couple of years back and we never had two cars on the road at the same time, so we let one go.

We know a couple of people who went bankrupt rather than pay off their debts. I thought about that, but it just didn't feel right. We paid off one of our credit cards this week that once stood at over $20,000.

Grand Poppa C and I shook hands and hugged. One down, three to go.

Talking of credit cards, you must never miss a payment by even a day, because it gives your credit card company an excuse to raise your interest rate to astronomic and impossible levels.

That's why I have such excellent credit (I know, the irony of it) because, and this bears repeating, I never miss a payment.

When I went to pay for the flights for me, Yaca, GAJ and Marley to come to Fiji to meet you for the first time (a glorious and rare phase when I had savings), my bank card kept getting rejected. The others were going to reimburse me, but we wanted to be sat together and I had enough money in the bank to cover it.

I rang City National Bank and was told that all purchases over $2,000 are automatically rejected as the majority of their customers have less than that amount in their accounts at any one time. This suggests that most Americans are just one month away from financial ruin or homelessness. Yikes.

That's one of the many wonderful things about living in Fiji, people don't starve. There are plenty of fish in the sea and fruit and vegetables growing wild.

Just got home from a meeting with my book lady who told me that she has such a lot on her plate at the moment and is so overwhelmed working for her family foundation and recording a new CD that she wants to put the book on the back burner. She realizes time is not on her side but that's her final decision.

The next day, I pulled into ABC Network for a pitch meeting for the TV show and parked under the giant Disney sign. I received a text from a couple who were looking for an English nanny to look after their baby girl part-time. They were looking for someone "practically perfect in every way."

I chuckled to myself as I passed all the photos from the Mary Poppins film in the corridor on the way to my pitch meeting. The babysitting job was clearly mine for the taking.

Against all odds, the couple went with a young mother who had a Masters degree in child development and used me as a back up.

Here's some advice: don't ever think things can't get any worse because they can and they often do. It's taking so long to get *The Bitches of Beverly Hills* picked up that two of the dogs have died, one owner doesn't want to be in it anymore and our gorgeous couple has separated. I am hiding under the duvet for a couple of hours then will get up, dust myself off, roll up my sleeves and get back to the business of life.

Life Lesson # 14 *If things aren't going according to plan, get off the pity pot and back to work because the harder we work, the luckier we are.*

Recommended further reading: *The Courage To Be Rich* by Suze Orman and *You Don't Have To Be Rich* by Jean Chatsky.

17

TOP TENS

I think you can tell quite a bit about someone from the books they like to read, the shows and films they like to watch and the music they like to listen to. I can't bear to watch violent or horror films, so my lists might be a bit tame for you. The following lists represent my own personal taste. Grand Poppa C urged me to include *Father Ted* in Top Ten Sitcoms. It is a constant source of disappointment to him that I don't find *Father Ted* remotely amusing. If nothing else, these lists will spark debate between you and your friends, family and future husband.

TOP TEN BOOKS

Act One by Moss Hart

To Kill a Mockingbird by Harper Lee

The House of the Spirits by Isabel Allende

Great Expectations by Charles Dickens

The Agony and the Ecstasy by Irving Stone

Angela's Ashes by Frank McCourt

One Hundred Years of Solitude by Gabriela Marcia Márquez

The Decline and Fall of Practically Everybody: Great Figures

of History Hilariously Humbled by Will Cuppy

Like Water for Chocolate by Laura Esquivel

Bossypants by Tina Fey

TOP TEN SITCOMS

M*A*S*H

Only Fools and Horses

Cheers

Frasier

The Big Bang Theory

Veep

Blackadder

Curb Your Enthusiasm

Friends

Modern Family

TOP TEN FILMS

The Shawshank Redemption

E.T.

Terminator 2

Cinema Paradiso

Like Water for Chocolate

Avatar

Parenthood

Mary Poppins

Some Like it Hot

Singing in the Rain

TOP TEN SONGWRITERS

Giacomo Puccini

Cole Porter

Irving Berlin

Lennon and McCartney

Joni Mitchell

Brian Wilson

Stevie Wonder

Bob Dylan

David Bowie

Julia Fordham

TOP TEN INSPIRATIONAL WOMEN

Marie Curie

Emmeline Pankhurst

Helen Keller

Annie Sullivan

Annie Oakley

Maya Angelou

Rosa Parks

Evelyn Glennie

Billie Jean King

Any mother who, despite centuries of cruel customs and ritual, refuses to allow her daughters (or sons) to have their genitals mutilated.

TOP TEN HOUSEHOLD HINTS

Pay someone else to clean your home

Pay someone else to clean your home

Pay someone else to clean your home

Pay someone else to clean your home

Pay someone else to clean your home

Pay someone else to clean your home

Pay someone else to clean your home

Pay someone else to clean your home

Pay someone else to clean your home

Pay someone else to clean your home

Life Lesson # 15 *Always wear rubber gloves if you have to do your own washing up and housework. It's why I have such soft hands.*

18

MY DAD

Your dad is the most brilliant, fun, loving, hands-on dad I have ever known. My dad comes a close second.

Mine taught me to catch a ball, play tennis and kick a football properly, which came in handy when your dad was a kid.

But everything stopped and we had to be dead quiet when the BBC news came on television at six o'clock. That inspired my interest in current affairs and a fervent desire to know what's going on in the world.

I remember being six years old and Dad patiently reading me the Rupert Bear cartoon in the *Daily Express* every day, even before he'd read the sports pages. He progressed to *The Independent* then the *Daily Telegraph* and would read me important stories out loud.

When I wrote a weekly column for *The Sun*, the UK's biggest-selling tabloid, he would buy a copy and hide it inside his (more serious) newspaper as he walked home from the newsagent. He was proud when I reported for his local BBC station.

He played hide and seek with us, and the ghost game, where he would look for us in the dark. When he found us under a bed, say, he would then shine a torch under his scary face for added shock and horror value. We screamed and roared with laughter.

When I was young, I could never open my mouth wide enough to get the first bite of the apple so I would hand one to him and say, "Dad, will you start my apple, please?"

He would take a large bite without saying a word or stop reading the newspaper and hand it back to me. I would eat the apple down to the core and hand it back to him to finish, seeds and all.

When I was nine, he sat through thirty versions of the song that started, "I Saw a Blackbird on Bluebird Hill..." I was 29th to perform in the singing competition and finished 7th. This was in the days when Dad was a chain smoker and he was truly desperate for a smoke by the end.

He was my hero. Still is.

Dad was an underwater photographer and worked for the Ministry of Defence most of his life. He'd go away on what were called trials and come back armed with gifts for us. Jewelry and exotic perfume for Mum: Joy by Jean Patou, Je Reviens by Worth, Estée Lauder, Yves Saint Laurent, Chanel. I would steal a spray of my favorites, Chanel No. 5 or Je Reviens, and play dress-up with my mum's jewelry. That's where I got the taste for nice things.

My dad was always game for a laugh and had a taste for adventure. I get that from him. I took him to Las Vegas for the weekend when he was 78, and he loves nothing more than going on the road with GAJ. We had a fabulous time in San Francisco when Dad was 83. Dad was awestruck by the redwood trees in Muir Woods. He loves nature. He marvels at everything.

He was always sporty and only recently stopped playing golf. His knees are no longer up to it.

The highlights and proudest moments of his life (excluding his children's achievements) were being Captain and President of Hayling Golf Club. We called him Captain and Mr. President for the duration of his times in office. The club is still the center of Dad and Mum's social life.

When we were kids, he played skittles, football, cricket and golf, but he didn't hang around in the pub after, just for half a bitter with the lads then home to his family, which was (and is) his everything. I have never seen my dad drunk.

I remember Dad taking me to watch him play cricket when I was about five. He explained the rules, showed me how to spin a cricket ball and practiced his stroke before his big moment. I could see he was nervous as he strode out to the wicket. He kept patting the wicket with the tip of his bat and readjusting his stance, holding up his finger to let the bowler know he wasn't quite ready.

He was bowled out for a golden duck (first ball). I heard him mumble, "Bollocks."

When I was three, my mum sent me to find out how Dad was getting on hanging the wallpaper in the hallway. I came back and reported his "it's like trying to hang pieces of shit."

My abiding memory of him is the time he and Mum were looking after an electric organ for a family friend. One morning we heard the sound of terrible playing coming from the living room. We all walked in to see dad sitting there buck naked, grinning as he looked over his shoulder at us *à la* Monty Python.

We kids howled with laughter. Mum walked out disgusted, mumbling, "Stop attention-seeking, Roy."

The closest I ever came to such comic genius (I love a visual gag) was when I did a naked Morris dance to make GAJ laugh when she was feeling a bit low. Naked as the day I was born apart from bells on my knees and handkerchiefs to wave − a perfect example of learned behavior.

My dad is the only man I can dance with the old-fashioned way. We used to dance together when *Come Dancing* was on the television. We made Mum laugh with our military two-step.

If I was bitten by a mosquito, Dad would spit and blow on it, any time of the day or night until it stopped itching. If I woke up in the middle of the night, he would make me butter balls covered in sugar. That might not have been such a good idea. Another perennial middle-of-the-night favorite was white bread soaked in hot milk and covered in sugar. It might be wise to get my arteries checked.

It was Dad who tucked us in and kissed us goodnight at bed time.

Fathers weren't present or welcome at the hospital during labor when I was a baby, so Dad cycled up the road to the public call box to find out if I'd been born yet. He cycled back down Bath Road with both arms in the air, the agreed signal if I was a girl. Nan, Grandpa and Uncle George were waiting outside the house for him. The neighbors clapped and cheered as he cycled by.

He cycled home from work for miles in torrential rain with a doll's house for me balanced on his handle bars. My mum reminds me of that on the rare occasion I moan about him.

He taught me to drive, and let me borrow his car once I passed my driving test. Before that, he drove me everywhere without complaint.

Dad told me (and only because I asked) that he was disappointed for a split second that I wasn't a boy.

His next-born was a boy, your Great Uncle Mark (GUM), so he did get a son to play and watch football with. They played golf and still play snooker together.

If anyone asks him when he was born, Dad answers, "April 27th, 1929. The day Portsmouth were beaten two-one by Bolton

Wanderers in the FA Cup Final."

In 2008, in Dad's eightieth year, Portsmouth (his local football team that he supported since boyhood and took me to see play at Fratton Park when I was a little girl) once again made it to the FA Cup Final. GUM took him to Wembley to see that historic game where Portsmouth (nicknamed Pompey) beat Cardiff by one goal to nothing. Dad didn't expect to live long enough to see Portsmouth win the FA Cup again after the last time in 1939. It was an added bonus in a long and happy life. I fancy Dad would have been almost content to die there and then.

Dad grew up during World War II and suffered food rationing and having his school friends and their homes blown to bits during frequent bombing raids.

If he hadn't been evacuated from Portsmouth as a boy during the war and left school at fourteen, as most of his contemporaries did, who knows what else he might have accomplished.

The deprivation and poverty he endured as a boy leaves Dad feeling appalled whenever future generations are offered meal choices rather than just eating what they are given. He also believes that modern parents worry way too much about their children's feelings being hurt over minor matters.

I was visiting my parents recently and we went to the local market. A street vendor was selling glue and shouting out to passers-by to buy his brand. Quick as a flash, Dad responded, "No, thanks. I'll stick with my usual brand."

My dad is the master of the pun and double entendre. I get my sense of humor from him. He's not perfect. He's not very good with money. He's the first at the bar to buy a round of drinks he can't afford. Lucky for him (for all of us), he has Mum to rein him in.

He needs a stick to lean on when he walks. He has chronic emphysema from years of smoking, diabetes and heart issues. He can still be shouty and impatient. He has mellowed with age, but still berates other drivers and waves his fist at them if they aren't, in his opinion, going fast enough.

He loves and lives for his family, planting flowers and growing vegetables in his garden, and feeding and watching birds.

After one terrible coughing fit, I asked him how old he was when he had his first cigarette. "Four," he said. He stole one of his dad's unfiltered Woodbines.

I asked him if he had any regrets in life. He thought for a while and said in all seriousness, "If I had my time over again, I wouldn't have bought my brown suit."

Despite decades of gentle suggestion that he answer the phone with a simple "Hello," he insists on saying "Good morning," "Good afternoon" or "Good evening" followed by the world's longest telephone number. Who still does that? My dad.

He asked me to send him a photograph of you to keep in his wallet to show his pals at the golf club. I sent him a fine selection. One of his last remaining wishes is to fly to Fiji to meet you in person.

I'm not sure he could handle that last leg of the trip in a tiny island hopper.

Nothing would surprise me with my dad, though. Fiji won't suit my mum for sure. She likes her creature comforts and plain food with gravy. Cockroaches the size of birds, moths the size of bats, spiders the size of dinner plates, frequent power cuts and the biblical tropical rains might be a bit much for her, too. They took a while for Yaca and me to get used to.

I think if my mum was presented with Anita's duck curry, complete with beak and feet, she would faint. I almost did. My dad would lap it up. I hope you inherit his taste and spirit of adventure.

Life Lesson # 16 *Your dad is the only man you know for sure will never stop loving you.*

19

DEATH AND DYING

Everyone dies. So please make the most of your life.

At the time of this writing, my dad and mum are still going pretty strong at eighty-five and eighty-one. This bodes well for you and me. It means we have good longevity genes. But we can't rely on genetic good fortune. Accidents happen, some folk will have disastrous diets, and sometimes people just have bad luck.

When my parents die, I hope they do what GAJ and I call an "Arthur Hall," and not an "Uncle George."

Arthur Hall was my dad's golfing buddy who died quickly and unexpectedly in his favorite armchair, aged eighty-two.

Uncle George, my dad's brother, was not so lucky. He had a massive stroke and stayed alive, barely, for eighteen months. He had full mental faculties, but was doubly incontinent and wore diapers. He was unable to speak, move or feed himself.

Three of my friends died slow and painful deaths from cancer, enduring the ravages of chemotherapy to prolong their lives for a few more miserable and desperate months, sometimes years, of suffering.

I am still reeling from the sudden death of my friend, Suzanne Krull. She died aged forty-seven of the same degenerative heart condition that killed her mother at the exact same age.

I can usually find something negative to say about most people, but Suzanne was that rare human who was loved and adored by everyone lucky enough to meet her. She was kind, funny, talented and loved life.

Suzanne was born with a number of painful and debilitating health issues. That's maybe why she loved life so much. She knew how fragile it is. She could have been bitter and angry, but she wasn't. Far from it.

I take some comfort from knowing she found true love with her husband, Peter, and they adopted a beautiful baby girl, Harper, so she knew the joy of the love between a mother and child.

Suzanne probably knew she might be dying after she became ill over the weekend. As she was being prepped for emergency surgery, she had enough time to say to Peter, "Tell Harper I love her."

I start crying all over again at the thought of Peter and Harper's pain and enormous loss. I don't know if Suzanne believed in life after death or if she's like another friend, Mary Herczog who knew she was dying and wrote her own eulogy where she asked that if anyone said at her wake, "God needed her more" we should punch them in the face.

Suzanne certainly hasn't gone to a happier place than her home with Peter and Harper. It was impossibly hard to say goodbye to her at her funeral.

Hundreds of us gathered at Mount Sinai Cemetery to celebrate Suzanne's life. We cried and we laughed. How Peter, heartbroken as he was, managed to raise so many laughs in his eulogy I'll never know. Well, he is a stand-up comedian but, nevertheless, his pain and sense of loss was palpable.

He told us the story of their first date at a coffee shop. He said he knew he wanted to marry Suzanne after the first sip of his latte. He decided he'd better wait until he'd finished his drink before proposing. With his usual, perfectly timed delivery, he said, "And I'm a man who takes a year to choose an electric toothbrush."

However unbearable it feels at the time, holding a service to celebrate the life of the departed is a vital part of the mourning process. It does bring healing. Eventually.

If a friend or distant relative dies in another country, GAJ and I go to the Self-Realization Fellowship in the Palisades off Sunset Boulevard to think about the lost loved one and share memories of them.

We don't go to the big temple, but walk around the stunningly beautiful and peaceful lake shrine with its amazing trees and flowers, fish, and swans floating by. The grounds include a court of religions honoring the five most popular faiths.

Right on the lake is a windmill with a tiny chapel. We go in there. GAJ offers up a prayer, and I meditate for ten minutes. We leave a donation in the box to help pay for the upkeep of this wonderful place. Then we have lunch or a walk along the beach. Life does go on.

If you're still living in Fiji when I snuff it, don't worry about flying in for my funeral. Just go to the beach at the bottom of Oneva, maybe go for a paddle and know that I loved walking along that beach with you. And know that I love you totally, utterly and unconditionally.

It may seem like you will never recover from the loss of a loved one, but you will. There are no rules about how long it should take to crawl out of bed and carry on with your life, but if you're still sobbing in the fetal position after six months, you need to get up and get busy — preferably doing something useful and beneficial to others.

That said, if anything happened to you, your dad or Yaca, I may never come out from under the duvet.

I only have a couple of regrets in my life. I bitterly regret not having done more for my grandmother, Nanny Fordham, to help ease her suffering when she was dying from cancer. GAJ and I went to visit her in hospital. She had tears in her eyes and asked us to speak to someone to see if they could do something about the terrible pain she was in.

GAJ was in her late teens and I was in my mid twenties. I wasn't as worldly wise and didn't have the confidence I have now, so I just asked the bored-looking nurse if she could give my nan something. That nurse couldn't have cared less about my grandmother or my request and carried on chatting to another nurse.

I felt I had done my bit by mentioning it and trusted the nurse would speak to a doctor, but knew deep down she probably wouldn't. Nan died a few weeks later. My dad assures me that he did sort out Nan's pain medication.

I won't let my parents down if they need an advocate. I will wrestle doctors and nurses to the ground until they do something and I don't mean just passing on a message or giving them an aspirin.

Apart from grandparents dying at a ripe old age, which never seems as terrible as someone who has young children, I haven't known many people who have died.

I told you about my friend Jenny who died aged forty from cancer leaving behind three young daughters being the inspiration for me to contact Grand Poppa C. Incidentally, Grand Poppa C also knew Jenny and attended her funeral. I had no idea they knew each other.

Anyway, Jenny's mum was very religious and wouldn't countenance the idea her daughter was dying, because that would mean she didn't have faith in God and he might ignore her prayers to spare Jenny.

Jenny felt the same, which is why she didn't write a will or say goodbye to her children. Her friends and family raised the $20,000 needed for her to fly from London to Mexico to a hospital that claimed they could cure her cancer.

GAJ and I went to visit Jenny at the hospital. One of her sisters was with her. Jenny had lost her hair through chemotherapy and, frankly, looked and felt dreadful. But she endured a raw fruit and vegetable diet and eight coffee enemas a day believing it would make her well again.

There were about fifty other stage-four cancer patients there who had begged or borrowed the money to pay for this last-ditch attempt to cling to life. The place was into shark and apricot stone capsules as a cure-all for cancer. Expensive, the doctors agreed (according to the video available in the lounge area), but proven, they claimed. I have one word: bullshit.

I asked some nurses and a couple of doctors if they kept records of patient survival rates, but once the patients had left after seven days they didn't keep track of them. There's a surprise.

Jenny died within a few weeks of leaving the hospital.

One day I will go back there undercover and expose those crooks that prey on the sick and desperate and steal (yes, steal) their money.

I have only been present at one death. It was the most traumatic experience of my life. GAJ's dog, Muttley, had been my nemesis when GAJ first brought him home as a puppy. It took a while, but I grew to love him and he was a member of our family.

GAJ found Muttley on a beach in Savusavu near where you live. He looked more like a bald rat than a dog. He was a starving, flea-ridden scrap of skin and bone. But because there's no rabies in Fiji, he breezed into America like an Arabian prince.

The vet in Los Angeles said he wouldn't live longer than a few weeks and certainly would always be a small dog if he did manage to keep going. Twelve years and sixty-five pounds later, Muttley kept losing his balance, so Julia took him to the vet, who diagnosed cancer. He was riddled with it. The vet wanted to put him to sleep there and then, but we asked for a stay of execution so we could spend a last weekend with him.

We gave him a send-off fit for the king canine he was. He dined on chicken and lamb chops. Friends came by to pay their respects and give him one last hug goodbye.

I didn't leave his side all weekend, stroked his back and scratched his neck for hours. I confess I was quite teary and wondered why people would choose to put themselves through this grief by having pets at all.

The vet came by the house to put Muttley to sleep. She assured us they often fall into a deep sleep as soon as she puts in the first needle. Occasionally, they last twenty seconds. Rarely, she said.

Not only did Muttley last longer than twenty seconds, he went for a stroll around the garden with the needle still hanging out of him. We chased after him and held him down while the vet put in the second needle. We gave him a lamb chop to chew on to take his mind off it. To cut a very long and upsetting story short, forty-five minutes and another shot later, still chewing his chop, Muttley finally gave up the ghost as GAJ, distraught, held Muttley and I held GAJ.

It was an absolute horror show that I never need to experience again. I thought GAJ would never recover from her loss. But she did.

We explained to Marley what had happened when she got in from school. Well, I did. GAJ was incapable of speech.

Marley, without missing a beat, said, "Can I have a kitten next?"

A neighbor, Mary Arden Collins, brought over some homemade vegetable soup and bread. It was the best part of the worst day. Take homemade vegetable soup or similar comfort food to the recently bereaved whenever possible. They will never forget your kindness.

Another friend and neighbor, India Redman, supervised the carrying off of Muttley's body by the VIP pet removal service, as GAJ and I were too upset. GAJ couldn't bear the thought that Muttley's body would be thrown into the back of a van. He wasn't, he was placed gently. I still miss him.

Carl and Shelley Randall have suffered seemingly unbearable loss in their lives, yet are the happiest most helpful citizens I know, always doing something for the Malibu community and their friends.

They live in a small apartment below a wonderful house facing the beach on Pacific Coast Highway. I mention they live in a small apartment because you might be thinking that living on the beach in Malibu, they can afford to buy things to help them more easily overcome their grief. They can't. Carl's sister, Julie, married Mark who became Carl's best friend. The devoted couple lived in Germany, but were home visiting for Carl and Julie's father's funeral.

Thirty-three year old Mark was putting out the trash cans when a driver took her eye off the notoriously busy PCH and crashed into him, killing him instantly. The family was devastated. Carl and Julie's mom, Carol, couldn't mourn her husband properly as she was busy comforting her daughter whose husband died so tragically within a week of her father.

Mark's funeral service was held the day after his father-in-law's.

Shelley told me, "It was terrible at the time. But you just keep going. You have to keep moving forward."

Shelley was adopted at birth into a loving family, but her mother died in a car accident that her father barely survived when Shelley was seven. He eventually re-married, an Egyptian hijab-wearing Muslim who brought blonde and blue-eyed Shelley up as her own. Shelley absolutely adores her.

Having spent some time with Shelley, I suspect she has been blessed with a happy gene, but we all have choices. Rather than feel rejected by her birth mother, she chose to be thankful she was adopted by a wonderful couple and doubly blessed when her father re-married another amazing woman.

Shelley said, "I don't have any sense or feeling of loss that my birth mother gave me up for adoption and I don't believe I've blocked the feelings. I think I was lucky to be adopted. I always knew I was adopted. I was always told I was chosen and I felt chosen. Children are often born knowing they were a mistake, or from an emotionally bad place such as to save an unhappy marriage. My adoptive parents had to make an enormous effort to go through the journey of adoption. Having the tragic loss of my adoptive mother, then having Mida, who loved me like I was her own child, I feel nothing less than blessed.

"Mida had her own son who was the same age as my brother, David. They were best friends. Then my father and Mida had their own son. Mida's son died some years later when he was forty, which was another loss for my family. Mida has never been the same person since her son died. But she has come back from the worst of her grief. That's the beauty of time and the beauty of life. You don't stay in that 'worst grief' state. Recovery from great loss happens organically. Of course, a child's death is more than anything any of us could ever bear. You lose a chunk of yourself that you will never get back. I remember thinking my mom is never coming back after her son died. But she did come back, although a piece is missing for sure."

Having her own child has made Shelley think about tracking down her birth mother. "Not because I want to start a relationship with her. Just to say thank you and let her know I'm doing fine. Better than fine."

Mia Rose, I just want to show you how we all have choices as to how we interpret potentially challenging and heartbreaking situations.

Not everyone sees things the same way as Shelley. Some adopted children carry a feeling of loss and abandonment all their lives. I hope I'd choose Shelley's take on it.

Talking of loss, after GAJ and I go to the Self-Realization Fellowship to mourn someone, we go over our own funeral plans to make sure the other is perfectly clear how we want to be remembered and have our bodies disposed of. We took a while to decide on our end-of-life care during many emotionally charged "what if?" discussions.

I don't want to carry on living if I am a Terri Schiavo trapped in a vegetative state, so please switch off the life support. Or a Christopher Reeve, where I still have all my marbles but am paralyzed from the neck down. GAJ eventually compromised: no to being kept alive like Terri Schiavo but yes to being kept alive like Christopher Reeve as she'd still have the same brain, heart and soul.

Terri was on life support for many years as her husband and parents argued through the courts whether or not she'd have wanted to have that life support switched off. If Terri had written what's called a living will, it wouldn't have been such an issue.

I suspect Terri would not have wanted her family to show film of her once-vibrant and beautiful self in a vegetative state as the nation debated her end. Just to be clear, no film of me on TV or the Internet looking anything less than vibrant and healthy, please.

I used to write about the importance of having a will during "Write Your Will Week" in the *Dorset Evening Echo*. Some PR agency would send out the prime worst-case scenarios if you don't write a will. There are differences in estate laws in every country, of course, but you'll get the gist and the potential for disaster.

Surely no one of sound mind would want to leave behind the financial chaos Stieg Larsson did? He's the Swedish author of *The Girl With The Dragon Tattoo* and the follow-ups that have gone on to make millions of dollars... for his father and brother from whom he was estranged. He hadn't written a will leaving his intellectual property to the woman he loved and lived with for almost thirty years.

How about the case of the elderly couple where everything was in the husband's name and they assumed the house would automatically go to the wife upon his death, so he didn't write a will? No. A niece and nephew who they had never met had a claim on a percentage of the value of the house. There weren't enough savings to pay them off and they insisted the house be sold immediately to give them their share, ensuring the grieving widow's last years were miserable and stressful.

When you write your will, you have to cover every eventuality. What if you and your spouse die in an accident? Who will look after your kids? What if you are all killed in an accident? If there isn't a will and a childless couple dies at the same time, the older of the two (usually the husband) is deemed to have died first and his wife's family could inherit everything while his family gets nothing.

If there's no legal document, it can take years to sort out an estate and cost a small fortune. While you're at it, you need to discuss with your family and state clearly in your will if you want your organs used for transplantation, the sort of funeral service you want, and if you'd want life support systems turned off.

Another useful tip: after years of working in television newsrooms, I have learned it's always a good idea to have a decent photograph of yourself looking your absolute best readily available in the unlikely event you win the lottery or are imprisoned, murdered or kidnapped, because the press will keep using whichever one they first lay their hands on and that's usually the one of you drunk at the office party or dressed in drag.

A fellow mourner was telling me at Suzanne's wake that her fiancée had been killed in a motorbike accident two years before, which was heartbreaking and devastating enough, but because she hadn't written a will, her three houses, her boat and not insignificant cash went to her mother who she hated.

I think I have proved the case beyond a reasonable doubt that dying intestate (without a will) is foolish and you never know when the end will come. You have to start by revoking all previous wills, mention all known children and beneficiaries by name and get your signature witnessed by two people. Best be clear that you want to leave your stocks and shares and the house in the Hamptons to the children you raised and not one you didn't even know existed.

One of the many advantages of being a woman is that you actually know how many children you've had. You'd be surprised how many men father children they don't know about.

I have written all my wishes in my last will and testament. Even if you only own a shell collection at this time, it can act as a template for you:

THIS IS THE LAST WILL AND TESTAMENT OF ME, CLAIRE RYAN, FORMERLY CLAIRE CROSS AND ALSO KNOWN AS CLAIRE FORDHAM OF [address].

1. I hereby revoke all previous wills and testamentary dispositions made by me.
2. I appoint my sister, Julia Fordham of [address] and my husband, Colin Ryan of [address] to be my trustees and executors. If Julia or Colin do not survive me, I appoint my son Max Cross to be my co-executor.
3. I bequeath the following legacies absolutely free of all duties and taxes:

My photograph albums to my sister, Julia Fordham.

The wedding photograph album to my husband, Colin Ryan.

My jewelry to my children Max and Mia Claire Cross. Specifically, my diamond engagement ring from Colin to my daughter, Mia. If they don't want it, then please give it to my grand daughter, Mia Rose Cross. It is of little value apart from sentimental.

There is a savings account in the name of Mia Rose, attached to my and Colin's Capital One Savings Account. I hope Colin will continue to save $20US into it (a monthly direct debit has been arranged from our bank account) to be used for education and adventures for Mia Rose as required.

All furniture, pictures and household items go to my husband, Colin Ryan.

4. Any income from my intellectual property shall be shared between the following:

10% to my parents, Roy and Muriel Fordham

50% to my husband, Colin Ryan

20% to my son, Max Cross

20% to my daughter, Mia Claire Cross

If my parents do not survive me, their share of my intellectual property will be apportioned between my children, Max and Mia Cross, giving them 25% each.

5. If my husband, Colin Ryan, does not survive me, his share of my property, possessions and any income from my intellectual property shall pass equally to my children, Max and Mia Claire Cross.

6. If my children do not survive me, their share of my intellectual property will go to their children. If my daughter Mia does not have children, 10% of Mia's share of my intellectual property will go to my sister, Julia, and that share to her daughter, Marley, on Julia's death. The remaining 10% (or 15%) if Mia does not survive me, will go to my son, Max.

7. In the event I am in a vegetative state, I do not want my life prolonged. Any life support systems should be turned off and I am not to be resuscitated if I have a heart attack or similar organ failure while in a vegetative state or if I have a terminal illness. If I am paralyzed from the neck down or suffering from "locked-in" syndrome, I do not want my life to continue unless medical science has by then progressed to the point of offering a full or substantive

cure.

8.   I request that my body be used after my death for
     therapeutic purposes (including corneal grafting and
     organ transplantation). That my remains be cremated in a
     simple wooden box, draped in red velvet. Single fresh
     flowers only from family members and garden posies
     from friends and well-wishers who may attend a simple,
     spiritual but non-religious ceremony and that my ashes
     be scattered in the sea at Santa Monica, California,
     followed by tea, cake and sandwiches somewhere
     convenient and inexpensive. Prosecco as well, if funds
     allow, to celebrate what has been the most amazing life
     where all my dreams came true. Finally, I ask that anyone
     who knew and liked me carry out a random act of
     kindness and think fondly of me as they do it.

Signed and dated by the above named Claire Ryan in our joint
presence and then by us in hers. Witnesses should print their
names and addresses and state their profession.

I met a death midwife. Who even knew there was such a thing? Just
as a birth midwife helps bring someone into this world, a death
midwife helps them depart from it. Olivia Bareham's mission in life
is to change the way we think about death.

"Most of us think death is a scary thing to be avoided at all
costs," Olivia said. "But watching my mother die completely
fearlessly had a huge impact on me. She knew where she was going
and she was ready."

When the hospice nurse in England invited Olivia to help bathe her mother's dead body, it sparked a desire in Olivia to help others die with the same courage, honesty and awareness as her mother.

Six months before she died of ovarian cancer, aged eighty-two, Rosemary Olive Bareham's doctor asked if she'd like to try another round of chemotherapy. She said, "No more of that nonsense, thank you."

"I cradled my mother as she cradled me as an infant, and I had this profound experience of love and continuity. After we bathed her body, we dressed my mother in her burial gown... ceremoniously, quietly, graciously and mindfully. The tears that flowed were not of grief but something cracking open. That's what I speak about in my workshops. It's this cracking open into a bigger place in our psyche that I want others to experience," said Olivia.

Now Olivia and others like her are reclaiming the lost art and healing rituals of a home funeral, which include conscious dying, bathing, dressing, anointing the body, laying it out in a place of honor and inviting people to look at the body to say goodbye.

This is not recommended if the deceased has died of Ebola fever.

Living in Los Angeles, Olivia has guided families through the many different religions, cultures, ideas and beliefs about death, "I respect all of them and have been involved in most. I hold open the space for the family to have the experience that they want for themselves."

According to Olivia, the ideal amount of time for a home funeral is three days, during which the body rests on dry ice to keep it refrigerated while the family builds a pine box or decorates a simple cremation casket. Olivia brings art supplies for the family to decorate the casket.

"It takes three days for the psyche of the bereaved to come to terms with the death. And to get the legal paperwork done," said Olivia. "Let's give ourselves three more days after death to experience and fully embrace what has just happened, then we can begin to accept our own mortality better."

Just so you know, neither GAJ nor I want our bodies to be on show in an open casket. No thank you. I'm not sure I even want my body in the house when people come round to pay their respects.

A dear friend had her husband's body taken away for cremation soon after his death, from cancer, and invited friends and family to visit for two hours over three nights and recall fond memories of the lost loved one. That's called Shiva in the Jewish faith. My friend isn't Jewish, but she liked the idea and it brought her great comfort to say goodbye that way. People took food and shared fond memories of the recently departed. I like that idea, too.

Your dad told me that funerals in Fiji are similar to the home funeral idea, although no consultants are used. The family bathes the body, often makes the coffin and digs the grave or builds the funeral pyre themselves.

199

After triple checking that I'm not breathing, just cremate me in a cheap cardboard box. Olivia assures me they can hold up to 200 lbs so there's no danger of me falling out the bottom.

When my Nanny Fordham died a few years after Grandpa Fordham, everything was left to Uncle George, as he had always lived with them and paid the mortgage when they bought their council house at 25 Bath Road, Southsea, Portsmouth, Hampshire (funny the things you remember). My dad was totally fine with that, but did ask George if he could have a memento to remember their mother by. George gave my dad their mother's toenail clippers.

I always found that amusing. My mum didn't. I have no idea if Auntie Joyce (Dad and Uncle George's sister) asked for anything, or what she was given if she did.

I doubt it was a framed photo of Nan and Grandpa, which is what my dad was hoping for, as George threw all the photos of them out because it was too painful for him to look at them. George never left the house again after Nan and Grandpa both died. He said it was too upsetting to go back into it when his mother, the last to go, was no longer there to greet him.

While we're on the subject, here's how I'd like to die: in bed while sleeping, aged ninety-six, holding hands with Grand Poppa C after a wonderful dinner with you and any other grandchildren I might be lucky enough to have.

I've recommended *The Tibetan Book of Living And Dying* by Sogyal Rinpoche for further reading. While I like the content and his easy style, I lost respect for him after I went to hear him talk in LA when I first arrived here. I was shocked and disappointed to see he dyed his hair black, when one of the main points of his book and Buddhist teaching is to let go of your ego. Frankly, that smacks of vanity and an enormous ego.

I mentioned this to my Buddhist friend, Monique Rhodes, who is a student of Sogyal Rinpoche, and she suggested my outrage over something so minor was more my problem than his. And anyway, she told me, he dyes his hair because his mother makes him. Mrs. Rinpoche dyes her hair and thinks her son should too. I'm still not convinced a man as spiritually advanced (allegedly) as Sogyal Rinpoche should dye his hair, but I concede it would be odd if he looked older than his mother, which he does with the white hair he has in his author's photo on my old copy of his wonderful book.

Life Lesson # 17 *Time is too precious to waste.*

Recommended further reading: *On Dying And Death* by Elisabeth Kübler-Ross, *The Tibetan Book Of Living And Dying* by Sogyal Rinpoche.

20

SIBLINGS

Your dad and Yaca fought like cat and dog when they were children. They were always squabbling and there was absolutely no love lost between them. This upset me greatly.

I had imagined my children would be the best of friends and play sweetly and lovingly together.

One time Yaca slammed the back door on your dad. He raised his hand to stop it and his hand smashed through the glass. I nearly fainted at the sight of all blood. Yaca felt terrible about it.

That was one of about forty trips to the ER between them. Most of their injuries happened during school sports but they weren't above punching each other or tripping the other up.

I turned to a friend for advice as she had kids the same age. She told me not to worry about mine as that very day one of hers had hit the other with a hammer. She was adamant that what my kids did to each other was tame compared to what hers got up to.

So I guess I was lucky your dad and Yaca didn't hit each other with weapons. Not that I know of, anyway.

They didn't really bond until we moved to London when they were aged 16 and 14. But they always had a shared love of extremely dark comedy and definitely became each other's support network when I moved to America. This was after they'd left home, but they continued visiting each other and speaking often by phone and reciting scenes from the film "Withnail and I" and the TV series "Bottom."

They helped me do a catering gig in Hollywood once and took great delight in offering the guests trays of food, "Cheesy dip?" They'd chorus and start giggling. They still do it.

The hardest they've ever laughed was when my mum walked into the living room one yuletide and announced she had laid a chocolate log on the dining room table. Now that was funny. Mainly because my mum didn't understand why we were all laughing.

Actually, the hardest they've ever laughed was when we all went to the Lake District to celebrate your Great Uncle Mark's 40th birthday. I was in one car with your dad and Yaca and GAJ was with our mum and dad in another. We kept missing the entrance to the restaurant and must have turned around six times, passing each other going the other way each time and then traveling miles in the wrong direction to find another turning space on the narrow and winding roads.

My dad and I were losing our minds by the end which only made your dad and Yaca laugh even more. Good times. That's what your dad and Yaca say to each other when they are especially happy.

Until you were born, your dad's sister was his favorite person. He loves and admires her so much that he bestowed the great honor of naming his first born daughter, Mia, after her. So you two get to call each other Yaca, which means namesake in Fijian.

That they have each other and love each other unconditionally is one of my greatest joys.

Watching them splash and swim together in the blue lagoon by your house in Fiji while I made sandcastles with you on the beach was bliss for me.

Blood isn't always thicker than water, though. I know siblings who haven't spoken to each other for years and don't get along at all.

My relationship with my sister, your Great Aunt Julia, is the longest and strongest I have ever known. She is my main confidante and I have shared many wonderful times and adventures with her.

We are each other's champion and protector. Good luck to the mister who comes between me and my sister.

I hadn't planned on writing a chapter about siblings. I think it has been well documented elsewhere in this book that I have a wonderful sister and so does your dad. But, as I write this in 2014, I have just learned that we are going to have a new family member.

I cried down the phone (happy tears) when your dad called me from the doctor's office to say the new baby he and your mom are expecting is a boy so you, too, will know the joy of a sibling's love and share the unique bond that can bring.

Named after his great-grandfather and grandfather, your brother Edward Isikeli is due to join our family at Christmas.

Life Lesson # 18 *Be kind to your brother. If you have a falling out, even if it's not your fault, say, "I'm sorry. Please forgive me. I love you." And hug it out. I wouldn't be so forgiving myself but this is my grandson we're talking about and I can't bear the thought of you two not getting along.*

21

THE POINT IS...

There have been articles floating around the Internet about how, when people are dying, their biggest regret is they wish they had spent more time living than working.

I rarely turn down an opportunity to meet a friend for lunch, play a game of tennis or hike, so that won't be an issue for me. I have no regrets, and feel I got the work/fun ratio right. If anything, I should have worked more.

But I've got better things to do. I love life. I also enjoy reading, especially self-help books. There's usually at least one grain of wisdom in each of them.

I've always been a fan of Dr. Wayne Dyer, a renowned self-help author and motivational speaker. In his latest book, a memoir, *I Can See Clearly Now*, Dr. Dyer explains how he believes there is a place within us all that, when nurtured and tested, gives us the power to live our lives at extraordinary levels.

In a universe that has no accidents, he says – a universe that is divinely orchestrated – miracles can be achieved and there are no limits to what we can accomplish if we tune in to "the powers of the invisible."

He has reached a new conclusion: rather than living our life with a "what's in it for me?" attitude, we should focus on "how may I reach out and serve?" Easy for him to say now he's made a ton of cash from his writing, but I do think he's right. The world would be a much better place if most humans weren't so selfish and stopped striving so hard to reach the imaginary "you can have it all" carrot that's constantly dangled.

Dr. Dyer recommends looking back over your life (once you've lived a bit) at key moments and the significant people who have helped you on your soul's journey. He says there is often a feeling of "things are meant to be" when we honor the calling deep within us.

As I look back on my life, I have no doubt that I was meant to be the mother of your dad and Yaca; your grandmother; GAJ's sister; Grand Poppa C's wife; Marley's aunt; and a writer living in LA. The number one thing I ever wanted was a family. I certainly have that. If this is as good as my life gets, I'm pretty happy with what I have achieved so far.

That assistant to a physical therapist job also had a lasting benefit for me. Twenty years ago, I tore the ligaments in my foot. My foot never healed properly and would swell up periodically if I was on my feet too much or driving for too long.

I limped into work one morning with my ankle strapped up and the physical therapist asked me what was wrong. After I explained, he said, "Do you suffer from back ache?"

I said, "Yes! Almost constantly. Getting out of bed in the morning is a nightmare and I can barely bend over to pick up a tennis ball without groaning."

"That's because the ligaments have healed 'short.' It impacts your back," he told me. "Do this exercise every day for a week and the pain will stop."

He was wrong. I only had to do the exercise for five days. Who'd have known an old ankle injury could impact your back? Should this happen to you, sit down and draw the alphabet in the air with your feet. It exercises all the muscles in the foot. Then place a rubber racket ball under your heel and press down for one full minute; then put it under the ball of your foot and press down, and hold for a minute.

My back ached for ten years. Not once since.

My needs are fairly simple and modest. I treasure philosophical discussions I have with GAJ over a cup of tea in the garden where we ponder the meaning of life. We also go for a morning walk together several times a week when we talk about everything and anything. I hope you are lucky enough to have such a trusted confidante.

On one of our hikes, as we trudged up a particularly hard hill, pausing to catch our breath and admire the view, I said I was disappointed that I hadn't arrived at a more positive conclusion about the point of life - that there is no point (my usual pronouncement). This is it. I had been hoping to offer more wisdom in this book.

GAJ suggested I meet an acquaintance of hers, Thea Nathan, a Reiki Master and death midwife. So we invited her to lunch.

Thea has a theory about the dangling carrot. She said, "We have been sold a myth. We've been striving for this perfect life. But nobody actually says: *It doesn't exist.* We're all striving for whatever it is that we think we're lacking. Everybody's life has some degree of suffering. It's part of the human experience. It can come at any point. I have found that the people who have suffered the most blows, where the rug has been pulled out from under them numerous times, are much more loving, kind and compassionate and live in the present.

"There's a quality to them that is real. Suffering is how you open to love. I wouldn't wish suffering on anybody, but when the heart has been broken over and over again, it stays open. There's not so much ego. The Eastern way of dealing with suffering is to fully embrace it rather than wanting a quick fix."

Thea feels she came into the world with an agenda to be at one with love and to know love. Not necessarily romantic love, but a deep spiritual love and connection to humanity.

I asked her if she thinks we have the power to change our own reality with our words and deeds.

"It's not black and white," said Thea, "but if it is for our higher good, yes. You can have things going well for a time, but something will come along. You might lose all your money or a loved one will die. All those things are pointers to finding love within yourself. Trust in the process of life."

I said, "Tell that to the 65 million people who died in World War Two, the 800,000 Tutsis and moderate Hutus massacred by Hutus in Rwanda, the more than 8,000 Bosnian Muslim men and boys killed by Bosnian Serb forces. Don't get me started on the Middle East."

Thea said, "The whys will never be answered. It will never make sense. Life will always deliver suffering to some degree. That in itself is humbling. There are millions of other horrible things happening in the world. I wish I could make sense of it. It will never make sense. For me, stopping striving and releasing the outcome has freed me up to just feel love."

"But we still have to take action. If Colin and I don't strive to earn money, then the rent won't be paid," I said.

Thea said, "Of course, if you get out there and are creative, more things are likely to come to you. If you are of service, things do seem to come to support you."

I told Thea about you and how you live in Fiji. She said, "I've been to Fiji. Fijians know about love. You can feel the love as you step off the plane. It's a soft and relaxing love. I loved talking to people there. They kiss and hug you when you meet them, so sweet and welcoming.

"There was fire-and-brimstone preaching at the village where I was, learned from the missionaries. But they still have that twinkle in their eye. Fijians are good, kind people."

Yes, they are.

I asked Grand Poppa C if he has any wisdom for you (and me) on the meaning of life? He said, "*Most discussions about life, the universe and everything usually boil down to two basic questions. Is it nature or nurture? Is everything predestined or is it all random and arbitrary?*

"The answer to the first one is usually 'a bit of both.' The second is more complex. Dr. Wayne Dyer believes in a universe where there are no accidents or coincidences, everything is worked out and even if someone is a tiny cog (metaphorically speaking) and can't see or even conceive of being an essential part of a greater mechanism, that grand design still exists.

At the other end of the spectrum, people will say things like, 'Hey, stuff happens and we all just have to deal with it. Adversity makes us stronger and wiser.' There might be a way to reconcile these opposing views.

"Religion, superstition and conspiracy theories are all manifestations of the same basic human need to superimpose an understandable pattern on what appears to be a chaotic universe. We want to believe that things happen for a reason, whatever that reason might be.

"The universe does behave according to various laws of physics that have been

tested and proven by some of humankind's greatest minds. Our knowledge is still limited, but one of scientist Sir Isaac Newton's findings is that for every action there is an equal and opposite reaction. He was thinking about matter in motion, although this could be applied to almost anything.

"Which brings us to karma, a 'spiritual' law that says everything we do, good or bad, has a wider effect on the universe, good or bad. Most people aren't really aware of karma. Who can blame them? Everyone is trying to make a living, bring up children, pay the bills and do the thousands of things that require our immediate attention every day.

"But what if we create karmic effects even though we're not aware of them? To use another metaphor, what if we all had a huge plank of wood balanced on our shoulder but paid no attention to it? What if we turned in this direction and that without any regard to how that plank might hit someone else or smash into things? Maybe that's why stuff happens and everything seems so chaotic and random.

"What if we were more mindful of this plank and behaved in a more enlightened manner? Perhaps the true design of the universe — if there is one — could unfold in a smoother way and perhaps humans could evolve to higher levels of existence where suffering is at least reduced."

That makes sense to me. It passes my smell test. By the way, Grand Poppa C's intelligence is one of the many things I find attractive about him. I hope you are lucky enough to find such a life partner, one who you fancy and who stimulates you intellectually.

My current conclusion is that there is a randomness to life from which no amount of positive thinking and goodly deeds will save you. But it's not worth wasting energy worrying about a disaster that probably won't happen, so we might as well think positively and be kind whenever possible. You, Mia Rose, are the mistress of your own destiny.

Thea has this advice for you, "Life is a magical mystery tour. Just enjoy the ride."

I'm not letting Thea have the last word. I am only half-joking when I say this, but I think the meaning of life may be as simple as the coconut macaroons I just made – perfect, just like you. I love you.

Life Lesson # 19   *Magical Mystery Tour? Life is a roller coaster! More fun than not though so do make the most of the good bits.*

Recommended further reading: *I Can See Clearly Now* by Dr. Wayne Dyer, *You Can Heal Your Life* by Louise L. Hay, *Autobiography of a Yogi* by Paramahansa Yogananda, *Fear Less* by Gavin De Becker.

22

FAVORITE FAMILY FOOD

British chef Jamie Oliver is doing much to improve the lives of children by encouraging healthy eating. He issued a challenge to all parents to teach their children how to cook and to encourage good eating habits because we are what we eat.

I think that's an excellent idea. Trouble is, once friends, family, gentleman callers and husbands realize you can cook, taking over that role can easily become a habit you might grow to resent. Make sure you cook because you want to, not because it's expected of you. Until you can afford your own personal cook, you will need to know a few basics to at least make it through college.

Eating a home-cooked meal with family and friends is my absolute favorite thing to do. I remember the first time I went to a dinner party, nearly forty years ago. The hostess was Kay Kerslake. Sadly, we've lost touch, but I can still remember that meal (pork cooked with cider, prunes and sage served with vegetables followed by a chocolate bombe) and realizing that food doesn't need to be just to fill you up, but a catalyst for good conversation and lots of laughter — as long as you don't discuss politics and religion or drink too much.

It can be expensive to host a dinner party, so to spread the cost you could ask guests to bring appetizers and/or dessert and you cook the main course. If money's really tight, serve pasta with a shop-bought pesto sauce, a green salad and crusty bread.

It's polite to take a bottle of wine to a dinner party if you are a guest, but never assume your guests will, so have a bottle or two ready. Serve water in a jug with slices of orange, cucumber, fresh mint and/or slices of lemon.

I like to have some appetizers available as soon as guests arrive. A nice paté served with cornichons (cocktail gherkins or leprechauns' willies as your dad and Yaca used to call them), a ripe brie or cambozola surrounded by pomegranate seeds or grapes and a bowl of hummus, all served with crackers and pitta bread. Grand Poppa C doesn't like hummus. He says it's like eating wallpaper paste with added garlic.

If you have guests joining you for dinner, always ask beforehand (not just as they're walking through the door, but days in advance) if they have any special dietary requirements or foods they can't abide. You'd be surprised how many people will forget to mention they have allergies to gluten or strawberries that are so severe it can result in a coma and sometimes even death. Or they think eating meat is murder.

Regarding gluten intolerance, my favorite gluten-free pasta is Quinoa (pronounced keen-wah) made by Ancient Harvest. I can't tell you how many brands of disgusting gluten-free alternatives I tried before I found one I liked. I swear no one will be able to tell it isn't regular pasta and even if you and your guests aren't gluten intolerant (like Grand Poppa C), most people will benefit and feel surprisingly not bloated after eating it. Quinoa flour for baking cakes works a treat too. Trader Joe's corn pasta is also good.

Grand Poppa C has been gluten-free for years and life became bearable again once I discovered gluten-free products I liked. Then Grand Poppa C decided to give that up for a week as well. So no gluten-free bread or pasta either. After just a few days without any grains at all (rice seems to be OK, though), his arthritis pain in his hands and knees disappeared completely and he stopped snoring. He now starts each day with a sliced-up apple and almond butter instead of gluten-free toast.

If you're a bit bunged up in the bowel department, eat some dried prunes or drink some prune juice. Not too much, though, as I gave you too much once when you were a baby and you had what can only be described as a nuclear and unrelenting poo.

Here are your dad and Yaca's favorite recipes that will help keep you happy, healthy, regular and popular. I've included my favorite desserts but, remember, pudding (or "afters" as we call it in England) is for special occasions only if you want to live a long and healthy life - unless you are a supermodel, of course, in which case you may have one teaspoonful of dessert once a year on your birthday. This is one of the many reasons I hope you don't become a supermodel. But, seriously, if you can't eat sweet things in moderation, don't have them in the house, and finish up celebratory meals with fresh fruit like the pineapple below.

SOUPS

Soups make a delicious appetizer or light meal and are easily made if you have a blender. You will have a blender because I am going to buy you one.

Take your favorite vegetables like broccoli, cauliflower, green beans, peas or carrots, cut them into small pieces and simmer until cooked in water, chicken or vegetable stock, salt and pepper and favorite fresh herb. Mint if it's peas, basil or tarragon for everything else. Let it cool and then blend and serve hot with a sprinkling of fresh herbs and a small dollop of cream provided you are not a supermodel and have no desire to be one.

Now, here's the thing: all soups taste better if you fry a small chopped onion on a low heat in a little oil and butter (a small spoonful of each as butter burns when you fry it on its own) until the onion is golden brown, then add the water or stock and chopped vegetable and cook until the veggie is soft. Stick it with a knife to check. If it goes in easily, it's cooked. Then blend and serve as above.

You can make a mixed vegetable soup to shake it up a bit and put everything you've got in it and leave the veggies in chunks rather than blend to really shake things up. This is more of what we call a hearty soup and equally delicious.

Once you become a more experienced cook, you won't need to be given exact measurements. Think about one-and-a-half pints of water or stock to a pound of vegetable. Maybe more if you like a thinner soup. Better to add more liquid to the soup once it's blended than have used too much in the first place. Practice makes perfect.

Salt and freshly ground pepper should be used in moderation, but add so much delicious flavor to everything.

Here's my absolute favorite soup recipe and the one I make once a week. But before that, here's an interesting fact: Yaca is repulsed by all hot liquids, including and especially soup. She is the only person I know who has never tasted tea, coffee or hot chocolate. I wish she felt the same way about diet soda.

For years, Yaca mocked my use of what she described as "compulsory garnish." Now she uses it too. I hope you will agree that a sprig of herb or drizzle of cream makes a dish much more attractive and appetizing. We're not animals.

ROASTED CARROT SOUP

Roasting the vegetables in the oven first intensifies their flavor.

Ingredients:

1 lb carrots

1 medium onion

1.5 pints vegetable or chicken stock or water and a stock cube will do (Chicken Oxo Cubes are my favorite)

Salt and pepper

Recipe:

1. Wash the carrots

2. Peel the onion and cut in half or quarters if it's a big one (I'll get you a pair of onion goggles – the best gift I ever bought myself to prevent onion juice getting in your eyes and making you sob into

the soup).

3. Place them on a non-stick roasting tin and sprinkle lightly with olive oil.

4. Toss them about and get stuck in with your hands to ensure an even coating of oil.

5. Lightly sprinkle with salt and pepper and some fresh or dried tarragon if you have any.

6. Cook in a medium oven around 325 degrees for about 45 minutes to an hour. Ovens vary but you'll want the veggies to be golden brown.

7. Place the carrots and onion, including all the scrapings from the tin, into a saucepan with the stock or water and simmer for ten minutes.

8. Allow the mixture to cool for a bit then pour into the blender and blend them together.

9. Re-heat with a splash of cream for added deliciousness then serve with your favorite bread or croutons.

COCONUT CHASER (FABULOUS FIJIAN APPETIZER)

Ingredients:

1 Fresh coconut

Zest and juice from 2 lemons

1 Fresh chili

Fresh ginger (about an inch-long piece after you've removed the skin, more if you especially like ginger)

Salt

Recipe

1. Thinly slice the coconut.

2. Wash the lemons and thinly dice or grate the lemon zest. Make sure you get all the white pith off or it will taste bitter.

3. Cut the lemons in half and using a fork squeeze all the juice out, discarding any pips.

4. Pound together with a mortar and pestle the lemon zest, juice, chilies, ginger and salt and thoroughly mix into the coconut.

5. Allow to stand for an hour, if you can stop yourself from eating it straight away. So simple, delicious and Fijian.

BOLOGNESE SAUCE

You can serve this with pasta and sprinkle with parmesan or any grated cheese, or top with mashed potato and brown off in the oven to make cottage pie (as pictured). Or add some chilies and chili powder when you brown the meat, and tinned kidney beans at the end to make a chili con carne, then serve with rice.

Ingredients:

1 lb of organic, grass fed minced beef, lamb or free range organic turkey

1 onion

1 carrot

1 stick celery

2 chopped garlic cloves

1 14-ounce can of tinned diced tomatoes

1 small can of tomato paste

Large splash of red wine, if you have any, or a splash of sherry. If I ever have any red wine left in a bottle (rarely, I admit) I freeze it in a little bag for sauces like this one

2 cups of chicken stock or water

Salt and pepper

A pinch of red hot chili pepper flakes

A small spoonful of sugar

Recipe:

1. Chop the onion and fry it in a little olive oil for five minutes.

2. Add the chopped carrot, celery and garlic and fry for a further ten minutes. I find this really enhances the flavor of the sauce. I tried just adding the chopped onion, carrot and celery to the browned meat to save on the calories, but it wasn't the same. It's not as good if you leave out the garlic either.

3. Add the meat and the chili flakes and cook the meat through.

4. Add the tomato paste and diced tomatoes. Stir thoroughly.

5. Fill the tomato can with water and add that and the splash of red wine or sherry if you have it.

6. Salt and pepper to taste

7. A teaspoon of sugar added to any recipe with tomatoes does wonders. Trust me on this.

8. Simmer for at least two hours.

CLAIRE'S CURRY

Ingredients:

1 large onion, chopped

2 garlic cloves

2 tbs coconut oil (unless cooking for Yaca who is repulsed by coconut oil so any oil but coconut. Don't try and fool her. She will know)

4tsp curry powder

1/2 tsp ground ginger

1/2 tsp ground cardamom

1/4 tsp cinnamon

1/4 tsp turmeric

1/2 tsp red chilli powder

1 tbs flour

1 x 14-ounce can of coconut cream

2 cups chicken broth

2tsp freshly grated lime zest

2lbs shrimp or fish, cooked chicken or turkey

2tbs fresh lime juice

Salt and pepper

Recipe:

1. Fry the chopped onion in the coconut oil until golden brown. Add the spices and flour and cook for one minute. If you don't have the extra spices don't worry, an extra tsp of curry powder will work. But these spices do add amazing flavors. And once you've bought them, they will keep for ages.

2. Stir in the coconut cream, chicken broth and lime zest. Bring to the boil and simmer for about two minutes, until it thickens.

3. Add the shrimp, fish or cooked chicken or turkey and bring back to a simmer for about five minutes.

4. Add the lime juice and salt and pepper to taste.

5. Serve the curry over cooked rice and top with chopped nuts, coriander and with Anita's Tomato Chutney as a side dish. I prefer basmati rice. This is enough for four to six main size servings, depending on appetites.

QUICK CURRY

Ingredients:

I large onion chopped or sliced

2 tbs coconut oil (see above regarding Yaca's repulsion)

2 jars of your favorite curry sauce

2lbs shrimp or fish, cooked chicken or turkey

Recipe:

1. Fry the onion and crushed garlic in the coconut oil in a heavy pan until soft and brown. This takes a while and requires constant stirring to prevent burning. It really tastes better when the onion is well cooked.

2. Add the two jars of curry sauce (I like Trader Joe's Thai Yellow). Bring to the boil and simmer for five minutes.

3. Add the shrimp, fish or cooked chicken or turkey. Bring to the boil and simmer for five minutes or until the fish is cooked and meat cooked through. This will feed six. Halve the recipe if cooking for two or three. I like cooking a big batch so you can eat it the next day and don't have to cook. It always tastes better the next day. Job done.

RICE

Rice is so easy to cook. For every one cup of rice you use two cups of water, add some salt to taste and simmer on a low heat until the rice has absorbed all the water, about 15 minutes. Brown rice takes much longer to cook but is much healthier. Check the instructions for brown rice as the water amounts vary. I add some peas (cooked from frozen from the start of cooking) for flavor and color.

ANITA'S TOMATO CHUTNEY

This is a perfect accompaniment for curry or fish (most dishes actually) - serve hot or cold.

Ingredients:

1 inch of peeled fresh ginger

1 chili

2 garlic cloves

1 tsp curry powder

Small onion chopped or sliced

Half a yellow or orange pepper chopped or thinly sliced

2 tbs coconut oil (unless Yaca's around obv)

1 14-ounce can of diced tomatoes

Recipe:

1. Crush the fresh ginger, chili and garlic cloves with a mortar and pestle. Put aside.

2. Fry the onion in the coconut oil until golden brown, then add the sliced pepper and cook for a further 5 minutes.

3. Add the ginger, chili and garlic mixture and cook for a few minutes so the flavors can mingle.

4. Add the tinned tomatoes and simmer for 15 minutes. Yum.

MASHED POTATO

This is the only dish that Grand Poppa C always makes. Everyone says his mashed potatoes taste better than anyone else's. He says it's the love we can taste. I had to ask him for his secret recipe to pass on to you. He wasn't sure he could trust anyone with it, not even you. Turns out, the secret ingredient isn't love but extra butter. I knew it.

Ingredients:

3lbs of potatoes

Splash of milk or cream

3ozs butter

Salt and pepper

Love

Recipe:

1. Peel, wash, quarter and boil the potatoes until soft. About 15 minutes. Don't let them get too soggy. Drain them in a colander and return to the pan.

2. Mash them together with the butter and milk or cream. Add salt and pepper to taste.

3. Add the love.

ROAST POTATOES

Ingredients:

3 lbs potatoes

1tbs flour

Olive oil, duck or goose fat

Salt and pepper

Recipe:

1. Pre-heat the oven on 375 to 400 degrees. It needs to be hot and ovens vary.

2. Peel, wash, quarter the potatoes and par-boil them for about 7 minutes. Unless you are in a real hurry, don't skip this bit as they do taste better for the boiling first.

3. Drain in a colander and sprinkle with the flour. Give them a

shake.

4. Heat the oil or fat in a non-stick baking tray, gently drop in the potatoes and lightly cover them in oil.

5. Check them after 45 minutes. Give the pan a shake and put them back in the oven if they're not yet golden brown and crispy.

SPANISH OMELETTE

Ingredients:

8 eggs

2 large or 3 medium onions

2 ozs butter and a large splash of olive oil

3 large potatoes

Grated cheese if desired

Salt and pepper

Recipe:

1. Peel and thinly slice the onions and fry in the butter and oil in a large frying pan or skillet on a low heat for around 20 minutes until they are golden brown.

2. Meanwhile, peel and cut the potatoes into biggish chunks and boil them for about 8 minutes until soft.

3. Drain the potatoes and add to the cooked onions. Fry them for a couple of minutes.

4. Beat the eggs in a large bowl, add the salt and pepper, and pour over the onions and potatoes. Sprinkle grated cheese on top if you like a cheesy omelet. Fry on a low heat. I add a lid to the pan so the omelet cooks through. Omelets this large are impossible to flip.

SALAD DRESSING

Ingredients:

3 parts olive oil

1 part rice or apple cider vinegar (I like rice vinegar)

Dijon mustard

Salt

Recipe:

Place all the ingredients in a clean glass jar, put the lid on and shake thoroughly. If it's a small batch, you'll just need a tsp of mustard. But if you're making a week's worth, more (obviously). Play around with the amounts. I like my dressing more vinegary, so I add a little more vinegar. You can add a whole garlic clove and keep it in the jar or lemon zest and juice. This will liven up and moisten your salads. Eat plenty of salad. It's quick, easy and nutritious. Unless you prefer a chopped salad like I do which takes longer to prepare.

MERINGUES

Ingredients:

Six large egg whites

12 ozs of caster sugar (granulated sugar in the US) – 2ozs per egg white for a smaller batch. Six egg whites will make about 20 small, like those pictured

1 pint whipped cream

Recipe:

1. Pre-heat an oven to 250 degrees.

2. Line a baking tray or two with parchment or baking paper.

Greaseproof paper won't do. This is where most people go wrong and the meringues stick to the paper.

3. Whisk the egg whites together in a large bowl until they form stiff peaks.

4. Fold in the sugar or whisk in on "low."

5. Take a tablespoonful of the mixture and place onto the tray using another spoon to ease it off. You can make lots of little ones or two giant plate-size ones and sandwich them together with cream and your favorite fruit. Or cover one with whipped cream and fruit for a classic Pavlova. I think making two large ones into a cake looks most spectacular. Just remember to spread both sides with cream.

6. Cook for two hours. Thanks to the parchment paper they'll come off easily once they've cooled for five minutes. Sandwich two together with whipped cream and arrange on your best plate. Stand by to become very popular indeed.

STRAWBERRY ICE CREAM

Ingredients:

1lb strawberries (Gaviota are the best)

3.5 ozs sugar

10 fl ozs whipping cream

Recipe:

1. Rinse the strawberries, remove the leaves and slice the fruit.

2. Cover them in the sugar and leave for an hour. Give them an occasional mix or shake as you go by.

3. Whip up the cream until thick enough to lie in folds rather than stand in peaks.

4. Zap the strawberries in a blender.

5. Fold the strawberry purée into the whipped cream.

6. Cover and freeze, checking and stirring the mixture as it freezes a couple of times, bringing the outside edges into the middle.

FRESH PINEAPPLE WITH MINT

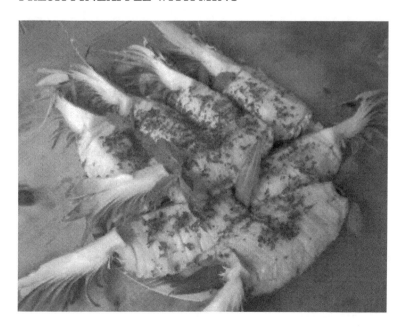

Ingredients:

1 ripe pineapple

Brown sugar

Fresh mint

Recipe:

Cut the pineapple into four pieces, keeping the leaves on for prettiness. Remove the core with a sharp knife. Then sprinkle with brown sugar and chopped mint. Serve quickly or the mint will go black. It looks spectacular and is delicious and refreshing. My friend Diane, who gave me the recipe, pounds the sugar (not much of it) and chopped mint in a mortar and pestle first, but I can't be bothered.

COCONUT MACAROONS

Ingredients:

3 large egg whites

½ cup sugar

½ tsp pure vanilla extract

¼ tsp salt

1 x 14oz packet sweetened shredded coconut

Recipe:

1. Heat oven to 325° F.

2. Line a baking sheet with parchment/baking paper.

3. Whisk together the egg whites, sugar, vanilla and salt in a bowl until glossy, foamy and the sugar is mostly dissolved.

4. Fold in the coconut until evenly combined.

5. Using a small ice cream scoop or mould the macaroons in your hand and place on the prepared baking sheet about 1 inch apart.

6. Bake for 20 to 25 minutes until golden brown, rotating the baking sheet about halfway through cooking.

7. Allow to cool before eating. They'll keep up to five days at room temperature in an airtight container. But they won't last that long.

Life Lesson # 20   *Favorite Food + Family = Happiness*

Recommended further reading: Any and all cookbooks by Delia Smith and Jamie Oliver, *Healthy Recipes* by Martha Rose Schulman, *Thirty Minute Meals* by Nigel Slater, *A Year at Otter Farm* by Mark Diacono.

My Darling Mia Rose,

I wish you courage to face your fears and lots of love. There is a peace and acceptance that comes with age, so I hope you live a long, happy, healthy, authentic, love-filled life. Thank-you notes and handwritten letters to friends and family who are grieving the loss of a loved one are important. Avoid buying plastic, be kind to the environment, people and animals. Don't get arrested and charged with a crime in Fiji, the UK or anywhere because you won't be able to visit me in America, let alone study, work or live here. That's not my rule, it's the US government's. I think I've just about covered everything. I love you.

Bubu

www.clairefordham.com

22117463R00141

Made in the USA
San Bernardino, CA
21 June 2015